The Rusty Parrot Cookbook

The Rusty Parrot Cookbook

RECIPES FROM JACKSON HOLE'S ACCLAIMED LODGE

Darla Worden and Eliza Cross

Photography by David Swift

GIBBS SMITH
TO ENRICH AND INSPIRE HUMANKIND
Salt Lake City | Charleston | Santa Fe | Santa Barbara

To my daughter Anna, a Rusty Parrot fan from way back. —DW

To my adventurous daughter Gracie, with fond memories of stargazing
from the Rusty Parrot rooftop. —EC

First Edition
13 12 11 10 09   5 4 3 2 1

Text © 2009 Darla Worden and Eliza Cross
Food Photographs © 2009 David Swift, as well as images on pages 2, 5 (bottom image), 14, 15, 26,
29, 35, 71, 76, 126, 145, 146, 179, 212, 216, 224
Additional photography © 2009 Jackson Hole Chamber of Commerce unless otherwise noted

Published by
Gibbs Smith
P.O. Box 667
Layton, Utah 84041

Orders: 1.800.835.4993
www.gibbs-smith.com

Design by Michelle Farinella Design

Printed and bound in Hong Kong
Gibbs Smith books are printed on either recycled, 100% post-consumer waste, FSC-certified papers or
on paper produced from a 100% certified sustainable forest/controlled wood source.

Library of Congress Cataloging-in-Publication Data

Worden, Darla.
  Rusty Parrot cookbook : recipes from Jackson Hole's acclaimed lodge / Darla Worden and Eliza Cross ;
photography by David Swift. — 1st ed.
    p. cm.
  Includes index.
  ISBN-13: 978-1-4236-0347-4
  ISBN-10: 1-4236-0347-8
  1. Cookery, American. 2. Rusty Parrot Lodge & Spa. 3. Jackson Hole (Wyo.)—Social life and customs.
I. Worden, Darla. II. Cross, Eliza. III. Title.
  TX715.B5625 2009
  641.59787'55—dc22
                        2008043314

CONTENTS

FOREWORD

When I was young, I loved waking up in that little attic room at grandma's and hearing her rattling pots and pans in the kitchen. Soon, the smell of fresh-baked muffins would drift up the stairs.

What a great way to start a day! Years later, those muffins came to play an important role in the creation of the Rusty Parrot.

After a visit in 1964 with a very gracious Bill Leavitt at the Alta Lodge in Alta, Utah, I decided that I wanted a small lodge at some time in my life. Bill had created a wonderful place. When you walked in, it just felt good to be there.

As the goal of a small lodge worked its way up the list, the memories of those muffins would come back. When we started to design the lodge, I felt there was no reason to go beyond a simple breakfast with hot, fresh muffins. Jackson had a lot of good restaurants. The smell of those muffins would be a great way to start the day; what more would we need or want?

As the Parrot has evolved, so has the food. We still have the same small kitchen that was designed for baking muffins. For the first twelve years, every chef we hired pleaded to do dinner, and I firmly said no. We were not about to do something that we couldn't do well. The small kitchen seemed an insurmountable obstacle. (By the way, even though we serve fresh muffins every day, we never did have just a simple breakfast. We changed that before our doors opened. How our culinary team creates the food it does in that kitchen is amazing.)

How and why we started doing dinner is a long story, but the short version is—it felt right. Staying in some wonderful small European inns with amazing food is a way to motivate anyone who loves the hospitality business. To us, good food, good wine, and good company all play an indispensable part of a great travel experience.

Over the years, Sandy and I set out to create a memorable experience in one of the world's memorable places—something we have thoroughly enjoyed. I hope we have succeeded in doing so with this book—that you will take home fond memories of an amazing place called Jackson Hole.

Live well, travel often, and occasionally overindulge. Moderation can be overdone.

—Ron and Sandy Harrison

ACKNOWLEDGMENTS

To Ron and Sandy Harrison, for sharing your vision of the Rusty Parrot and for your help with and support of this book—not to mention generously sharing family recipes.

To Jim Promo, class act extraordinaire, who never complained no matter how tedious our questions were and who worked to squeeze in photo shoots, author visits, and test recipes during the Rusty Parrot's busy schedule.

To affable photographer David Swift, for the stunning images you shot, for your expertise before, during, and after the photo shoots, for your happy attitude—and for introducing us to the Flight of the Conchords.

To Jeffrey Blackwell and the entire culinary staff at the Rusty Parrot, for adjusting and testing your amazing recipes and for preparing dish after breathtaking dish for several lengthy photo shoots.

To Anne McGregor Parsons, WordMaster extraordinaire, for your perfectly targeted suggestions and gentle corrections.

To Lauren Whaley, for helping with so many details and for your "can-do" attitude and sunny presence during several long days of shooting images.

To Heather Petty, for painstakingly transcribing the recipes.

To the cooks and staff at the Wild Sage and Rusty Parrot Lodge & Spa, for your help and support throughout the project.

To MJ, for being the embodiment of hospitality, a warm and welcoming presence at the Rusty Parrot.

To Kim Walkenhorst, for enthusiastically testing the elk recipes; and to Kent Walkenhorst, for providing the main ingredient.

To Catherine Bauers, for sharing your treasure trove of beautiful tablecloths.

To Heather Falk and Maureen Murphy of the Jackson Hole Chamber of Commerce, for loaning us a cache of Jackson photos.

To Lisa Watson, for sending incredible shots of Jackson Hole Mountain Resort.

To Amanda Flosbach of the Grand Teton Music Festival.

To our editor, Jennifer Grillone, for bringing your in-depth editing experience and aesthetic sense to this project.

And finally, to Gibbs Smith—for having the vision and wherewithal to bring this book to life.

INTRODUCTION

Jackson Hole's Historic Roots

Surrounded by towering mountain ranges, Jackson Hole, Wyoming, was originally named by fur trappers who coined the term "hole" to describe the encircled valley floor. They called it "Jackson's Hole" after area fur trapper Davy Jackson—and the moniker eventually was shortened to Jackson Hole.

At a time when homestead claims were up for grabs across the U.S., Jackson Hole's geographic isolation, altitude, and harsh climate discouraged early settlement. But in 1883, President Chester Arthur and his entourage made an extended tour of northwestern Wyoming, trailing down the Gros Ventre River into Jackson Hole and then into Yellowstone. Word spread of "the Hole's" unique beauty, abundant game, and proximity to Yellowstone, attracting the first brave homesteader to stake a claim in the valley in 1884.

The area's dominant winters—with the first snow appearing as early as September and the last flakes falling in June—made proving up a homestead challenging. Spring and fall offer beautiful-but-short seasonal transitions, and summer temperatures rarely exceed the 80s. As homesteaders once said, "If summer falls on a weekend, let's have a picnic."

Still, settlers were optimistic about their new life in Jackson Hole. Some tried growing crops of potatoes and hay despite the short season, while others attempted cattle ranching—a livelihood that has endured in the valley for some 130 years.

Jackson's remote location proved a challenge to pioneers, who depended on supply centers located over the pass in Idaho, near the rail line, for goods and necessities. Freighters, companies that transported goods from Idaho over Teton Pass and through the valley, proved the pioneers' lifeline, and they depended on reliable transportation. Still many hazards arose to delay or prevent delivery of goods—dangerous river fords, skittish horses, and avalanches in winter. The establishment of reliable transportation routes into the valley was a prerequisite to Jackson Hole becoming a successful settlement.

Many homesteaders lived at a subsistence level, surviving on odd jobs and whatever crops they could produce. Some left the area's harsh winters to return in spring, a pattern that still continues with Jackson's summer residents. Others bolstered incomes with trapping or outfitting and guiding East Coast "dudes"; the emergence of the first dude ranch in 1907 created a new type of job in the valley.

Prompted by curiosity about the American West, attracted by the majestic beauty of Jackson Hole and its ruggedly dramatic Teton Range, and curious to explore Yellowstone, the nation's first national park, tourists began arriving at the Victor, Idaho, railway station and securing coaches over Teton Pass into Jackson. The advent of the automobile in the 1920s forever changed Jackson from a predominantly agricultural community to a tourism-centered one.

Early tourist facilities in the area ranged from tents to simple log cabins for hunters who hired Wyoming guides to take them on adventures in the fall. Business-minded settlers figured out that if visitors were willing to rough it every fall, why not provide them with a family-travel opportunity, and many dude ranches were expanded with cabins and lodges where East Coast dudes could spend the entire summer with their families.

To support the emerging tourism industry, lodges, hotels, roadhouses, and dude ranches sprouted in the valley. That tradition continues today, with numerous lodging options catering to the millions of visitors who come for the area's beauty, skiing, and wildlife, as well as a glimpse of the Old West still alive in Jackson Hole. It is within this tradition of welcoming hospitality that the Rusty Parrot Lodge & Spa, Jackson's quintessential in-town luxury lodge, presides.

Rusty Parrot Origins

Entrepreneur Ron Harrison founded the Rusty Parrot in 1990 after extensive travel and personal observation of high-end lodging properties all over the world. Intentionally tailored to its Jackson setting and located within walking distance of the Town Square's many shops and restaurants, the intimate thirty-one-room lodge was designed with a comfortable, timeless Western ambience. Well-appointed rooms include in-room fireplaces and Jacuzzi baths, one-of-a-kind handcrafted furniture, and down comforters.

Jackson's Playground—Grand Teton National Park

When visitors fly into Jackson Hole Airport, the only airport in the country located in a national park, they enjoy a perspective of miles of unspoiled open range and sagebrush-covered valley floors with little discernible development until they reach the town of Jackson. These wide-open spaces are the result of the foresight of John D. Rockefeller Jr.

When Rockefeller and his wife visited in 1926, they were dismayed by what they saw—Jackson Hole's magnificent landscape, particularly around Jenny Lake, was becoming overdeveloped and chopped up with many unsightly commercial developments. To preserve the area's rich natural beauty, they created the Snake River Land Company and purchased more than 35,000 acres—of which 32,419 were eventually donated and incorporated into Grand Teton National Park. In 1929, congress created Grand Teton National Park, comprising most of the mountains and forever changing the history of the valley.

The Rockefellers' generous legacy continues through the present with the November 2007 announcement by the National Park Service of another gift. The 1,106-acre Laurance S. Rockefeller Preserve, located on the shore of Phelps Lake, has been conveyed to the National Park Service. The Preserve, formerly known as the JY Ranch, is one of the most pristine, scenic, and wildlife-rich areas of the park. John D. Rockefeller Jr. purchased the ranch in 1932, intending to include it in a sizeable land donation to the park. Over the years, however, it became a treasured family retreat and remained private property. Laurance inherited the JY from his father, and in the 1990s, he arranged for the transfer of a significant portion of the ranch—some 2,000 acres—to Grand Teton.

Grand Teton National Park attracts visitors who appreciate its quiet beauty. Unlike the "Broadway" of Yellowstone, with it's fanfare of showstopping geysers and spectacular waterfalls, Grand Teton National Park is more "ballet at Lincoln Center," with outstanding performances from the scenery of the Teton Range, Jenny Lake, and the Snake River Oxbow. Grand Teton National Park also serves as Jackson's official playground—a mere four miles from town.

Winter Home on the Range—The National Elk Refuge

As many as 25,000 elk ranged in the valley when the first settlers arrived in Jackson Hole. The arrival of settlers quickly impacted the elk's habitat; the Town of Jackson was built on a large portion of the elk's wintering ground and settlers' homesteads pushed elk out of their traditional winter habitat, forcing them to compete with livestock for food. In the early 1900s, the elk population suffered a serious setback when severe winter storms created deep crusted snow. The National Elk Refuge was created in 1912 out of public concern for the elk, to protect what was considered the largest herd on earth.

Today, administered by the U.S. Fish and Wildlife Service, the National Elk Refuge preserves 25,000 acres of winter range (approximately a quarter of the herd's original range). On an average, 7,500 elk seek winter refuge here, staying around six months. The current migration route of the herd is from southern Montana to the refuge area, and it remains the longest migration route of any mammal in the lower forty-eight states. An eight-foot-high fence along the main highway and the northern border of town prevents elk from moving through Jackson and onto private lands, protecting them from encounters with automobiles and humans.

Yellowstone National Park—Jackson's Famous Neighbor

When John Colter (credited as the first non–Native American to visit Yellowstone country) returned to Missouri with his tales of boiling mud and steaming water rising from the ground, no one believed him. It was only years later in 1871, when the U.S. Geological Survey sponsored a trip to Yellowstone—this time including naturalists, geologists, a landscape artist, and two photographers—that what had seemed tall tales were proven true. Armed with pictures and photographs when they returned, the expedition offered evidence of their wild stories about the area, and in 1872, the U.S. Congress declared Yellowstone the country's first national park.

Located just seventy-five miles north of Jackson, Yellowstone National Park encompasses 3,472 square miles located in three states—Montana, Idaho, and Wyoming—with the majority of the park in Wyoming. Known for its spectacular geothermal features—geysers, mud pots, and hot springs—Yellowstone also draws travelers to view its rich array of wildlife, including grizzly bears, wolves, bison and elk. (Curious fact: More people are injured by bison than by bears each year.)

As the nation's most popular national park, Yellowstone attracts nearly three million visitors each year to glimpse its magnificent attractions, including Old Faithful, the Grand Canyon of the Yellowstone, and Yellowstone Lake.

As one of the gateway cities to the park, Jackson remains a popular stopping point for tourists on their way to and from the park.

Today: The Town of Jackson

Just plain "Jackson" is the name of the town—located within the Jackson Hole area that encompasses Grand Teton Park, Teton Village, and the small towns of Kelly, Wilson, and Moose. Established in 1901, Jackson remains a symbol of the Old West, with its old-fashioned wooden sidewalks, elk antler arches on the Town Square, famous Cowboy Bar with neon bucking bronco sign and saddle barstools, and a real rodeo each summer.

From its Wild West beginnings in the early 1900s, the town's population has grown to more than 8,000, and despite many changes during the years, much has stayed the same. Summer is the busiest time of year, one of the favorite topics of conversation is still the weather, and tourism has remained Jackson's primary industry.

Known as the "Gateway to Yellowstone," Jackson is a short drive from Grand Teton and Yellowstone National Parks. The town also serves as home to a world-renowned ski resort—Jackson Hole Mountain Resort. Each year millions of visitors arrive to enjoy the spectacular sights and activities of the area.

Each season brings something new for locals and guests to anticipate: The Old West Days of spring, Music in the Hole on the Fourth of July, the Jackson Hole Fall Arts Festival, and the largest sled dog race in the lower forty-eight states during the recently dubbed "dog days" of January.

By the end of activity-filled days, visitors seek a comfortable bed and a memorable meal to complete their Jackson Hole experience—which is where the Rusty Parrot comes in. Located just minutes from the Town Square, this lodge is Jackson's gem. Acclaimed by *USA*

Today as the best place to snuggle in front of the fire, and by *Ski* magazine as one of the best small hotels, the Rusty Parrot Lodge & Spa was named number-one hotel in the continental U.S. and Canada by *Travel + Leisure* magazine readers in 2005. The Rusty Parrot's restaurant, Wild Sage, has received AAA's Four-Diamond rating since 2004 and has won numerous awards and accolades. It has been featured on the Food Network, in the *New York Times*, *Elle Décor*, the *Chicago Sun Times*, *Cowboys & Indians*, and was included on *Mountain Living* magazine's Top Mountain Restaurant list.

    Jackson Hole's seasons are extreme and the location is remote, so the Rusty Parrot strives to make guests comfortable whatever the outdoor elements bring; and Wild Sage features menus dictated by the weather—comfort food in the chill of fall and winter, lighter fare through spring and summer—incorporating local and fresh ingredients year-round.

    One thing is certain, Jackson leaves a mark on those who visit as a place they won't soon forget.

Photo credit: Tristan Greszko/JHMR

Cowboy Bards

Cowboy poetry dates back to cattle drives following the Civil War. Many of the country's first cowboys came from Anglo-Saxon, Celtic, and Gaelic roots in the British Isles. Known for their traditions of balladry, these cowboys amused themselves on cattle drives by sharing songs and poems from their homeland, creating early cowboy poems that were a combination of Irish storytelling, Scottish seafaring, and cattle tending. The image of cowboys sitting around a campfire telling tales and reciting poetry has become an iconic image of the American West.

The Rusty Parrot honors Jackson Hole's tradition of working cowboys by introducing guests to a different poem each evening at turndown service. Choosing from a repertoire of excellent regional and traditional cowboy poetry, the Rusty Parrot places a poem on guests' pillows along with a chocolate treat to ensure sweet dreams.

The Cow Puncher

He rides the earth with hoofs of might,

His was the song the eagle sings;

Strong as the eagle's his delight,

For like his rope, his heart hath wings.

Owen Wister
Author of *The Virginian*
Jackson Hole, 1903

Parrot Tales—How the Rusty Parrot Got Its Name

When owner Ron Harrison was searching for a name for his new Jackson lodge, he wanted something to reflect the unique nature of the property that would be easy to remember when people recommended the lodge to their friends. He put together a long list of possibilities then narrowed it down by eliminating any name using the words "Jackson," "Teton," or anything suggesting arrival on a covered wagon. With a short list in hand, he took one final road trip to visit with innkeepers of some of the best small hotels in the country.

Over the years, the name has been the subject of a lot of speculation. Soon after opening, the Rusty Parrot held a community-wide contest to see who could come up with the best story about the name's inspiration. The winning entry was a fully illustrated tale depicting the plight of all the bedraggled animals of Jackson Hole. It told the sad stories of the Mangy Moose, the Blue Lion, the White Buffalo, the Lame Duck, and, of course, the Rusty Parrot. The poor outcast animals all settled in welcoming Jackson, where they could live in harmony and without persecution, and enjoy the area's natural beauty.

Some tall tales about the name have evolved, some pretty interesting. If you want the whole story of how and why, the only way you can get it is to corner Ron and get him to relate it to you. For now let's just say that there is a Rusty Parrot and he resides in Jackson Hole.

P.S. The old parrot has lived a life of comfort at the lodge. He oversaw operations from a prominent perch in the lobby for many years. He now has a private room where he can enjoy the fruits of his labor.

Wild Sage

The Wild Sage has often been called the heart of the Rusty Parrot Lodge & Spa. At once comfortable and elegant, the restaurant is an intimate gathering room that beckons guests from the main entrance of the lodge. A wood fire crackles in the river-rock fireplace surrounded by soft leather couches that invite conversing and relaxing. Handcrafted wood furniture and Western art create a warm ambience, and soft lighting illuminates hundreds of bottles of wine from the Wild Sage's collection displayed in custom wall racks. With just twenty-six seats, the restaurant offers a cozy, intimate dining experience.

The restaurant has provided a full breakfast since the lodge opened in 1990. Each morning, the smells of fresh-brewed coffee and an appetizing breakfast waft through the inn; guests help themselves to hot coffee and fresh-squeezed juices at the counter and select muffins, fresh fruit, granola, and yogurt from a laden sideboard. The daily made-to-order breakfast offerings are posted on a blackboard on the wall and might include such temptations as fresh-from-the griddle flapjacks accompanied by Wyoming huckleberries and barrel-aged maple syrup, or creamy polenta enlivened with fresh tomatoes and basil and topped with spinach, poached eggs, and a homemade champagne cream sauce. In the afternoon, coffee, tea, and homemade cookies are ready for guests returning from the ski slopes, hiking, or other activities.

The Wild Sage began serving dinner in 2000. From the imaginative menu and diverse wine list to the thoughtful, unobtrusive service, Ron Harrison's vision was to enhance the guest experience by creating an unparalleled restaurant at the inn. A favorite with locals and dignitaries alike, the Wild Sage serves bistro-style entrées that change seasonally, featuring heartier fare in the autumn and winter months and lighter offerings in spring and summer. The executive chef and culinary staff prepare regional cuisine with fresh, organically grown produce; naturally raised game, fowl, and meats; sustainable fish and seafood; and freshly baked breads, pastries, and desserts.

Top-quality ingredients, a talented staff, an inviting dining room, the freshest meats and produce, seafood flown in daily, a wide-ranging wine list, and a sophisticated menu with some unexpected surprises—these elements are all hallmarks of the Wild Sage experience.

Dice

Mince

Chiffonade

Julienne

Brunoise

About the Recipes

The Wild Sage kitchen is compact, and its size dictates that cooks practice careful organization and preparation; the French use the term *mise en place*, or "put in its place." While many of the recipes in this book are quite complex, home cooks can utilize a similar discipline by reading the recipes through to get a sense of timing required for each step, by assembling the ingredients in advance and by gathering the necessary cooking implements prior to cooking. When the recipes call for unusual ingredients, refer to the Resources section at the back of the book for retail sources.

General ingredients guideline

Butter: use unsalted butter

Cream: use heavy whipping cream but preferably not "ultra-pasteurized," as the higher processing temperature dulls the flavor

Eggs: use large eggs at room temperature

Flour: use all-purpose flour unless otherwise specified

Salt: use table salt or sea salt unless otherwise specified

Sugar: use granulated sugar unless otherwise specified

Vanilla: choose pure vanilla extract, not imitation

The baking recipes were tested at the Rusty Parrot kitchen's elevation of 6,200 feet and may need to be adjusted for other altitudes.

Many of the recipes call for ingredients to be prepared by chopping or cutting in small pieces. Always use a sharp chef's knife with a wide stiff blade for chopping and slicing. The knife techniques referenced in the recipes are illustrated on the right.

SPRING SURPRISES

Always Hungry

Gray fluffs that beg at my closed sill,

The size of seconds, never still.

They coax and tweet you out of eats,

Like growing boys, these chick-a-dee'ts.

Jessa Eula Wallis

Laramie, 1923

EVEN WINTER'S LOYAL FANS greet spring in Jackson enthusiastically. The season begins subtly: woods creaking with the thaw, the creek splashing against rocks, purple hyacinths and yellow daffodils pushing out of snow.

Some of the more skeptical residents refuse to believe spring has arrived—snow has been known to fall in June. But as the days get warmer and longer, Jackson's residents and visitors launch into action—determined to enjoy each passing moment. As soon as it's possible to hit the trails in hiking boots or hop on a bike for a ride, you'll see people in Jackson outdoors.

Perhaps the official harbinger of spring here comes in April in Grand Teton National Park. The Park Service closes the road to motorized vehicles but sweeps it clean for bicycles and rollerblades, creating, if only temporarily, the best bike path in the country beneath the spectacular Cathedral Range. Then in May, the road opens to cars, making it possible to drive to the Tetons' many lakes and trails, providing additional opportunities for outdoor adventure.

Traveling to nearby Yellowstone National Park to observe the newborn bison, grizzly cubs, and wolves is another rite of spring. Yellowstone's Lamar Valley, considered an American Serengeti for its wildlife-rich habitat, provides prime viewing of nature at her finest.

IN MAY, THE WHOLE TOWN OF JACKSON comes out for ElkFest and Old West Days, two events that provide a lively connection with Jackson's past. For ElkFest, the Jackson Hole Boy Scouts host a famous Antler Auction, selling antlers they've harvested from the National Elk Refuge. The only event of its kind, ElkFest draws buyers from around the world to bid on the impressive pieces, shed naturally by elk that winter on the refuge.

Held over Memorial Day Weekend, Old West Days offers activities that include gunfight reenactments in the Town Square, the Jackson Hole Rodeo, a fine wine tasting at the Jackson Hole Rotary Wine Fest, a Western and English tack and gear swap, a Mountain Man "Traders Row," and a rendezvous of vendors showcasing handmade elk antler wares. The highlight of the weekend includes the Memorial Day Parade, the largest horse-drawn parade in the country, which attracts the local folks, who come out to honor our veterans and say "hello" to neighbors they haven't seen all winter.

The Wild Sage welcomes springtime each year with a new menu that

emphasizes the season's fresh produce and lighter fare. Even though snow showers may continue well into early summer, thin stalks of bright-green asparagus, tender pea shoots, baby lettuces, and fresh herbs begin to appear in the markets and make their way onto the menu.

Winter's hearty soups and stews are replaced with lighter broths and soups, and edible flower blossoms begin to show up on the restaurant's complex salads. Fresh-caught fish such as salmon and tuna are carefully prepared to highlight delicate flavors, and desserts celebrate the increasing availability of sun-ripened fruits and just-picked berries.

Wolf Watch

When the West was settled, the eradication of the gray wolf (*Canis lupus*) was considered a marker of civilization; in Wyoming, the gray wolf was officially eliminated in the 1930s. Then in 1995, keeping with Yellowstone National Park's goal of perpetuating native species and their habitat, the National Park Service reintroduced fourteen gray wolves from western Canada to Yellowstone's Lamar Valley to repopulate and restore nature's balance of wildlife.

Today, the number of wolves in Yellowstone and nearby Idaho has grown to about 1,300, but the reintroduced animals continue to be controversial. Whatever decisions are made outside Yellowstone's borders, wolves remain protected inside the park, which will continue to serve as a safe harbor for the packs in the future.

Since the wolves' reintroduction, wolf lovers from around the world have been drawn to Yellowstone's Lamar Valley in spring and fall for a glimpse of wolf packs in their natural habitat. A short drive from Yellowstone, the Rusty Parrot provides guests with a magnificent opportunity to enjoy the park's natural predators each spring with its "Wolf and Grizzly Safari." This three- or four-night expedition takes guests into Yellowstone during prime viewing season for glimpses of grizzlies, black bears, and wolves roaming the park's evergreen forests and rolling meadows. The trip has proved one of the Rusty Parrot's most popular guest adventures.

MAKES 4 TO 6 SERVINGS

FOR THE OIL

1/4 cup extra virgin olive oil

1 ounce fresh thyme sprigs

FOR THE GARNISH

1 tablespoon salt

1 quart water

1 pound fresh asparagus, trimmed,
    cut diagonally into 2-inch pieces,
    tips reserved

2 ounces speck ham, julienned

FOR THE SOUP

6 cups chicken stock

2 teaspoons salt

3 leeks, diced (1/2-inch cubes),
    white part only

4 cloves garlic, peeled and minced

3 tablespoons cornstarch

1 cup heavy cream

PURÉE OF SPRING ASPARAGUS
with Thyme Oil and Crispy Speck Ham

Infused with the flavors of a spring garden, this rich creamy soup is topped with crunchy Italian dry-cured speck ham and a swirl of fragrant thyme olive oil.

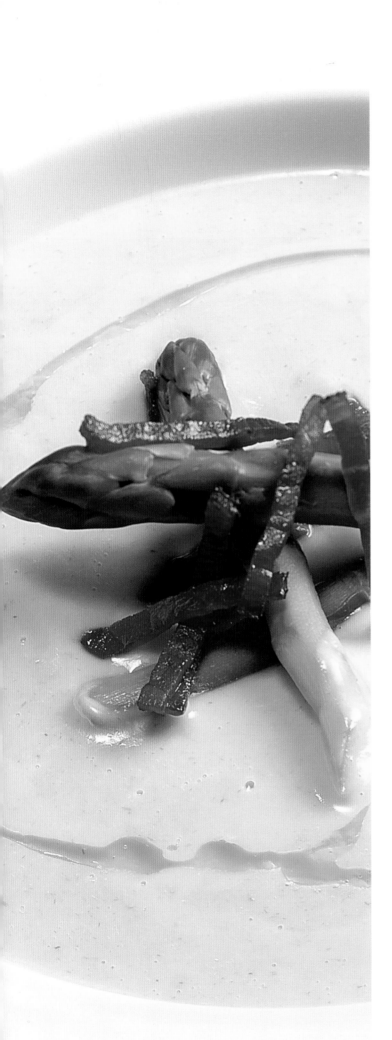

To prepare the oil: heat the olive oil in a heavy saucepan over low heat. Add the thyme and steep for 10 minutes. Remove from heat, cool, strain, and set aside.

To prepare the garnish: add the salt to the water in a medium saucepan and bring to a boil. Blanch just the asparagus tips for 30 seconds; drain, and set aside. Heat a large saucepan over low heat and add the speck ham. Cook for about 6 minutes, or until the fat is rendered and the ham is lightly browned; drain and set aside.

To prepare the soup: heat the chicken stock in a medium saucepan and add the salt, the rest of the asparagus, leeks, and garlic; bring to a simmer. In a large bowl, combine the cornstarch with the cream and whisk until blended. Add the asparagus stock to the prepared cream and stir until blended. Return the mixture to the pan and bring to a simmer; remove from heat.

To serve the soup: ladle into bowls; garnish with asparagus tips and speck ham.

MAKES 4 TO 6 SERVINGS

FOR THE CREMA

1 tablespoon buttermilk

1 cup heavy cream

1 tablespoon finely chopped
    lemon zest

FOR THE SOUP

10 vine-ripened tomatoes

1 shallot

6 cloves garlic

2 tablespoons canola oil

1 quart water

FOR THE GARNISH

1 teaspoon truffle oil

2 tablespoons fresh basil chiffonade

ROASTED VINE-RIPE TOMATO SOUP
with Lemon Crema and Fresh Basil Chiffonade

This summery soup—made with ripe garden-fresh tomatoes—
is rich and colorful. Roasting the tomatoes highlights their
rich flavor, and a swirl of lemon-infused cream offsets the
acidity and creates a nice contrast in the bowl.

To prepare the crema: combine the buttermilk and heavy cream a day before and mix well. Let stand loosely covered overnight at room temperature. The next day, add lemon zest and set aside.

To prepare the soup: preheat the oven to 350 degrees F. Core and cut each tomato in half, peel the shallots and garlic, toss in canola oil, and then roast on a sheet pan for 20 minutes. Peel the skin from the tomatoes. In a small saucepan, combine the tomatoes, shallot, and garlic; add the water and reduce by one-third. Purée in a blender.

To serve the soup: ladle into bowls, drizzle with crema and truffle oil, and garnish with basil.

FOR THE PEARS

2 cups Muscat wine

1/2 cup sugar

4 cups cold water

1 vanilla bean, split

1 cinnamon stick

2 star anise pods

3 D'Anjou pears, peeled, halved, and cored

FOR THE VINAIGRETTE

1/3 cup white balsamic vinegar

1 clove garlic, peeled and minced

1 shallot, peeled and minced

1/2 teaspoon salt

1/4 teaspoon ground white pepper

1 tablespoon Dijon mustard

1 tablespoon sugar

2/3 cup canola oil

1 tablespoon white truffle oil

FOR THE JAM

1/2 medium red onion, peeled and finely julienned

1/2 cup Chianti vinegar

1/2 cup sugar

1/8 teaspoon salt

PEA SHOOT SALAD
with White Truffle Vinaigrette, Red Onion Jam, Maverick Farms Flatiron Steak, Chimichurri, Saga Blue Cheese, and Muscat-Poached Pear

Tender pea shoots are sometimes found at farmers markets in the spring and fall, and can also be harvested from pea plants in the garden. Choose shoots that include the delicate tendrils and tender leaves from the top of the plant. The greens pair well with D'Anjou pears simmered in sweet Muscat wine to balance their tart undertones; the plate is finished with chimichurri, an Argentine herb-based sauce.

FOR THE CHIMICHURRI

1 cup packed, chopped fresh parsley (stems removed)

1/4 cup packed, chopped fresh cilantro (stems removed)

1/2 shallot, peeled and minced

1 teaspoon lemon juice

1/2 cup grapeseed oil

1/4 teaspoon salt

FOR THE STEAKS

3 (6-ounce) Maverick Farms flatiron steaks

1 teaspoon salt

1/2 teaspoon freshly ground black pepper

2 tablespoons canola oil

FOR THE SALAD

1 cup fresh pea shoots

FOR THE GARNISH

2 ounces Saga blue cheese, crumbled

To prepare the pears: reduce the wine by half in a tall-sided saucepan over high heat, cooking off the alcohol. Add the sugar, water, vanilla bean, cinnamon stick, anise pods, and pears to the liquid; cover with a coffee filter. Cook the mixture until it comes to a boil. Remove from the heat and refrigerate the pears in the liquid overnight.

To prepare the vinaigrette: add all the ingredients except the oils and process in a blender until smooth. Slowly add the oils so they emulsify into the mixture; strain and set aside in the refrigerator.

To prepare the jam: combine all the ingredients in a small saucepan and heat over medium-high until simmering. Cook until the mixture is syrupy and reduced by half. Remove the mixture from the pan and refrigerate.

To prepare the chimichurri: combine all the ingredients in a blender. Process the mixture for 20–30 seconds, or until herbs are finely ground.

To prepare the steaks: preheat the oven to 375 degrees F. Remove any sinew from the meat. Season both sides with salt and pepper. Add the oil to a sauté pan over high heat; sear the steaks on both sides. Finish in the oven for 3–5 minutes. Remove the steaks from the oven, top the meat with a healthy portion of the chimichurri, and then let the meat rest for 4–6 minutes.

To serve the salad: remove the pears from the liquid and arrange them on the upper left side of each plate. Toss the pea shoots in a small amount of the vinaigrette, just enough to coat evenly. Slice the steak on the bias and place over the edge of the pea shoots. Top with some of the red onion jam and Saga blue cheese. Garnish the plate with the remaining chimichurri.

MAKES 6 SERVINGS

FOR THE DRESSING

3 bacon slices
2 dried chipotle peppers,
    finely ground
1/2 teaspoon salt
1 lime, juiced
2 tablespoons sour cream
5 tablespoons mayonnaise

FOR THE RELISH

4 Roma tomatoes, diced
    (1/4-inch cubes)
1 shallot, peeled and minced
2 tablespoons fresh cilantro
    chiffonade
1/4 teaspoon salt
1/4 teaspoon lime juice
2 jalapeño peppers, seeded and
    minced
1/2 cup dry turtle beans, cooked
    and cooled
2 fresh corn ears, shucked, roasted,
    and kernels removed

FOR THE HEARTS OF PALM

3 cups canola oil
3 ounces fresh hearts of palm
1/3 cup flour
1/2 teaspoon salt, plus extra for
    seasoning
1/2 teaspoon finely ground
    chimayo chile

BABY SPINACH SALAD
with Sweet Corn and Turtle Bean Relish, Chipotle-Lime Dressing, Enoki Mushrooms, and Chile-Dusted Hearts of Palm

This fresh interpretation of the classic spinach salad pairs baby spinach, fresh corn, tender beans, and crispy fried hearts of palm with a creamy dressing enlivened by chipotle peppers and lime juice.

FOR THE SALAD

9 ounces baby spinach

FOR THE GARNISH

Enoki mushrooms, trimmed
    to 2-inch lengths
Tortilla crisps

To prepare the dressing: slice the bacon into 1/4-inch julienne. In a small sauté pan over low heat, render the bacon until crisp. Drain on paper towels and reserve the bacon fat. In a mixing bowl, combine the warm bacon fat, chipotle, and salt. Add the lime juice, sour cream, and mayonnaise; mix well to combine. Pour the dressing in a plastic squeeze bottle and refrigerate until ready to serve.

To prepare the relish: combine all the ingredients in a small bowl and stir gently; refrigerate until needed.

To prepare the hearts of palm: heat the oil to 325 degrees F in a heavy saucepan. Slice the hearts of palm crosswise on a mandoline to 1/8-inch thickness. Combine the flour, salt, and chile in a mixing bowl. Toss the hearts of palm in the flour mixture and coat well. Fry the hearts in the oil until crisp and golden brown. Drain the hearts on a tray lined with paper towels; sprinkle the hearts with a little salt.

To serve the salad: arrange spinach in the center of the plate; top with relish and dressing. Sprinkle with bacon and mushrooms, and add additional relish, if desired. Garnish with a squeeze of dressing on the plate, hearts of palm, and a tortilla crisp.

MAKES 4 SERVINGS

FOR THE GELÉE

1/2 cup Verjus Blanc
1/2 tablespoon agar agar
1 tablespoon sugar

FOR THE POTATOES

3 cups water
1 teaspoon salt
8 Russian banana fingerling
   potatoes
1/2 teaspoon truffle oil

FOR THE HARICOTS VERTS

3 cups water
1 teaspoon salt
2 tablespoons fresh basil chiffonade
1/4 pound haricots verts

FOR THE TOMATOES

1 quart water
1 teaspoon salt
4 purple Cherokee tomatoes
4 Zebra Stripe tomatoes
4 Marvel Stripe tomatoes
4 yellow Teardrop tomatoes

FOR THE TUNA

14 ounces tuna, portioned into
   4 (1/4-inch-thick) steaks

WILD-CAUGHT AHI TUNA NIÇOISE SALAD

with Olives, Haricots Verts, Fingerling
Potatoes, Heirloom Tomatoes,
and 12-Year Balsamic Vinegar

The classic niçoise salad is taken to new heights with
sashimi-quality fresh tuna and straight-from-the-garden
fingerling potatoes and baby tomatoes.

FOR THE GARNISH

3 ounces pitted niçoise olives
3 ounces pitted kalamata olives
1 teaspoon fleur de sel (sea salt)
2-1/2 teaspoons 12-year balsamic
   vinegar
1 tablespoon extra virgin olive oil

To prepare the gelée: combine the Verjus, agar agar, and sugar in a small saucepan and let stand for 10 minutes. Bring the mixture to a boil, strain through a fine mesh sieve, and pour into a pan to a 1/4-inch depth. Chill in the refrigerator until set. Cut into 1/4-inch squares when ready to serve.

To prepare the potatoes: heat the water and salt to a simmer in a small saucepan. Add the potatoes and cook for about 20 minutes. Cool potatoes in an ice bath. Once cool, toss in the truffle oil.

To prepare the haricots verts: heat the water and salt to a simmer in a small saucepan. Place the basil chiffonade in a cheesecloth purse. Add the basil purse and beans to the water and cook for 2 minutes. Remove the beans from the pan and cool in a water bath; discard the basil purse.

To prepare the tomatoes: put the water and salt in a small saucepan and bring to a simmer. Using a sharp knife, cut a small X on the bottom of each tomato. Add the tomatoes to the water and cook for 20 seconds. Place the tomatoes in an ice water bath and cool. Remove the skin from each tomato, cover, and refrigerate.

To serve the salad: place tuna in the center of the plate. Arrange potatoes and haricots verts around the tuna. Garnish remaining areas of the plate with olives and tomatoes. Season fish with salt and gelée. Finish the plate with drizzles of balsamic vinegar and olive oil.

A Landlocked Fish Monger

The seashore may be miles away from Jackson, but fortunately there's a local fisherman with a passion for quality who flies in the freshest fish from both coasts. Jack Goldstein is the owner of Hole Fish Company, the commercial purveyor that supplies the Wild Sage as well as other restaurants, caterers, food service companies, and private chefs in the Jackson Hole region. "I get the biggest kick out of bringing the best seafood I can get to folks who love seafood but couldn't otherwise purchase it locally," Goldstein says. "We fly seafood in directly from suppliers around the country, and we work hard to source seafood from U.S. fisheries that support locally based fishermen."

Hole Fish Company's suppliers promote using sustainable catching methods and fishing gear that target specific species without disturbing the marine environment. Goldstein is also committed to supporting local community-based fishermen and their families.

The Wild Sage kitchen offers sustainable, wild-caught fish species whenever possible, and Goldstein says he often calls the restaurant when he gets unusual offerings. "The Wild Sage chef is always interested in our seasonal specialties and unique seafood items," Goldstein says. "Some of the restaurant's signature menu dishes have been developed from several fish varieties we offer, like Wild Alaska Ivory King Salmon and Yellowtail Hamachi."

For regular folks in the Jackson Hole area, the company also offers its fresh fish at the retail seafood service counter at locally owned supermarket Jackson Whole Grocer and ships select products directly online from its retail website, Bristol Bay Seafood (bristolbayseafood.com).

FOR THE CRAB CAKE MIX

2 eggs

1 tablespoon Old Bay seasoning

2 tablespoons Dijon mustard

1/2 cup mayonnaise

1 tablespoon freshly squeezed
lemon juice

FOR THE CRAB CAKES

1 pound jumbo lump crab

1/2 cup panko crumbs

6 tablespoons canola oil

FOR THE COULIS

2 corn ears, roasted

1 clove garlic, peeled and minced

1 shallot, peeled and chopped

1 cup heavy cream

1 cup chicken stock

1 teaspoon salt

1 tablespoon sugar

FOR THE REMOULADE

2 egg yolks

1 clove garlic, minced

1 tablespoon lemon juice

1 cup canola oil

1 tablespoon packed
chopped parsley

Pinch of salt

1/4 teaspoon chimayo chile

1 pickled fennel bulb

JUMBO LUMP CRAB CAKE
with Sweet Corn Emulsion, Alligator Pear Relish, and Fennel Pickle Remoulade

"Alligator Pear" is another name for avocado; some say it's because the tough leathery peel resembles the skin of an alligator. These tender, oversized crab cakes served with a rich corn coulis and avocado salsa are one of the most popular appetizers at the Wild Sage.

FOR THE RELISH

2 avocados, peeled and diced (1/4-inch cubes)

1 large vine-ripened tomato

2 tablespoons cilantro

1/2 lime, juiced

1 shallot, peeled and finely chopped

1 jalapeño, seeded and finely chopped

1/8 teaspoon salt

Microgreens for garnish

To prepare the crab cake mix: combine all the ingredients in a small bowl and measure out 1/2 cup. Discard the remainder or use for another purpose.

To prepare the crab cakes: preheat the oven to 350 degrees F. Mix the crabmeat and breadcrumbs with the crab cake mix; chill in the refrigerator for 1 hour. Form into 4 cakes. Heat the oil in a large, heavy sauté pan over medium-high heat. Sauté the crab cakes until golden brown. Finish in the oven for 4 minutes.

To prepare the coulis: combine all the ingredients in a heavy saucepan and cook over medium-high heat until the mixture simmers and is reduced by about one-fourth. Cool, then purée in a blender or food processor. Strain the mixture through a fine sieve and set aside.

To prepare the remoulade: add egg yolks, garlic, and lemon juice to a food processor and process. While running slowly, emulsify the oil and then add parsley, salt, chile, and fennel; mix thoroughly and refrigerate.

To prepare the relish: combine the ingredients in a small bowl.

To serve the appetizer: using a 2-1/2-inch ring mold, portion the relish into 4 servings and pack down. Remove the mold and place a crab cake on top of the relish. Spoon a dollop of remoulade on top of the crab cake. Drizzle the coulis around the cake and garnish with microgreens.

Wine Pairing Ramey Hyde Vineyard Chardonnay, Carneros, Napa Valley, California; or Roessler Cellars Clos Pepe Chardonnay, Santa Rita Hills, Santa Barbara, California

Tasting Notes The richness and fatty components of this dish need a fuller-bodied wine with significant acidity to cleanse the palate between bites; the wine also has to be rich enough to stand up to the food's main components.

MAKES 6 SERVINGS

FOR THE OIL

2 ounces fresh chives,
   chopped (1/2-inch pieces)
1 cup canola oil

FOR THE RELISH

3 ounces lump blue crabmeat
1 tablespoon finely
   minced chives
1-1/2 teaspoons lemon juice
1/8 teaspoon salt

FOR THE HOPPIN' JOHN

6 cups water, divided
1/3 cup dry black-eyed peas
1 teaspoon salt
3 tablespoons canola oil
3/4 cup diced yellow onion
1/4 cup red bell pepper brunoise
1/2 cup diced peeled carrot
1/4 cup diced peeled parsnip
1/4 pound Basque chorizo
1 cup vegetable juice
   (such as V-8)
1 teaspoon Chimayo chile powder
1/2 teaspoon salt

FOR THE BATTER

2 egg yolks
1-1/4 cups cold sparkling water
1 tablespoon sake
1/2 cup flour
1/2 cup cornstarch

KEY WEST SHRIMP TENDON, BLUE CRAB, AND CHIVE RELISH, "Hoppin' John," and Serrano Ham

A popular dish in the South, Hoppin' John is the American version of rice and beans made with black-eyed peas, rice, and tomato. Here it's paired with a jumbo shrimp wrapped in savory Serrano ham and fried in a light, crispy tempura batter.

FOR THE SHRIMP

1 quart canola oil
6 Key West shrimp (8–12
   count per package), peeled,
   deveined, and butterflied
6 ounces Serrano ham,
   cut into paper-thin slices
4 tablespoons flour
12 sprigs fresh chives
   for garnishing

To prepare the oil: put the chives and oil in a blender and process for 30 seconds. Pour the mixture into an airtight container and refrigerate for 24 hours. Strain through a fine chinois and let drain for 1 hour (do not push on the solids); set aside.

To prepare the relish: pick through the crabmeat to remove any tiny pieces of shell and debris, leaving all lumps as intact as possible. Combine all the ingredients in a small bowl and stir gently. Refrigerate until needed.

To prepare the Hoppin' John: put 2 cups water and the black-eyed peas in a large saucepan and soak for 6 hours. Add the remaining water and the salt, and heat over medium-high heat until the mixture comes to a simmer. Cover and simmer for 1 hour; remove from the heat and cool; drain and discard the cooking water.

In a large skillet, heat the canola oil over medium heat and cook the onion, stirring occasionally, until golden brown and caramelized. Add the bell pepper, carrot, parsnip, and chorizo, and cook until tender. Add the black-eyed peas, vegetable juice, Chimayo chile, and salt. Simmer for 5 minutes, reduce heat to low, and keep warm.

To prepare the batter: beat the egg yolks in a medium bowl and add the sparkling water and the sake. Stir until just combined. In a separate bowl, combine the flour and the cornstarch. Add the flour mixture to the egg mixture, stirring just until blended. Do not overmix.

To prepare the shrimp: preheat the oil to 350 degrees F in a heavy, tall-sided pot. Stuff approximately 2 teaspoons of crab relish into each shrimp and wrap in a slice of Serrano ham. Dust each shrimp with flour and then dip in the tempura batter. Fry 2–4 minutes, turning once, until the shrimp is done; drain briefly on paper towels.

To serve the appetizer: spoon some of the hoppin' John on the center of each plate. Using a sharp knife, cut each shrimp on the bias into 3 pieces. Arrange the shrimp on top of the Hoppin' John, drizzle with chive oil, and garnish with chive sprigs.

Wine Pairing Domaine Tempier Bandol Rosé, Bandol, Provence, France

Tasting Notes There are many different textural and flavor profiles in this dish: the tempura-fried tendon stuffed with the blue crab and chives, the spiciness of chorizo, the earth components of root vegetables in the Hoppin' John, and the richness of the Serrano ham. This rosé is a great pairing due to its richness.

Wines of the Wild Sage

Considering the intimate size of the restaurant, the Wild Sage has a surprisingly large and wide-ranging wine list. Between 150 and 200 individual wines are offered, and the restaurant cellars approximately 3,000 bottles. Accordingly, the Wild Sage has been the recipient of the Wine Spectator Award of Excellence for numerous years.

The wine list offers a diverse representation of wines from the finest producers and wine-growing regions around the world. The list includes a broad sampling of varietals and appellations—including vintages from well-known wineries as well as lesser-known, off-the-beaten-path wines—for the Wild Sage's guests to experience. Sparkling and dessert wines are also offered as well as ports, cognacs, liqueurs, and other spirits.

Part of the sommelier's charge is to create a synergy between the seasonal Wild Sage menus and the wines that accompany the food, highlighting the flavors of the cuisine and matching them to the wines. Along with assisting guests in their wine choices, the sommelier also tastes everything that goes on the wine list and develops the descriptions based on his or her personal evaluation.

The executive chef and sommelier are encouraged to attend wine tastings together, and the Harrisons often travel with the general manager, executive chef, and sommelier to experience different cuisines and wine in a variety of cities and settings. The ultimate goal is that all guests of the Wild Sage enjoy a highly personalized culinary and wine experience that exceeds expectations.

MAKES 6 SERVINGS

FOR THE SAUCE

3 cloves garlic, peeled and minced
1 shallot, peeled and minced
1 tablespoon champagne vinegar
1 cup white wine
1/2 cup orange juice
2 egg yolks
1 cup clarified butter
1/4 teaspoon salt

FOR THE QUINOA

1 quart water
1 teaspoon salt
1 cup quinoa, rinsed and strained

FOR THE VEGETABLES

2 tablespoons butter
1/2 cup finely diced onion
1/2 cup finely diced celery
1/2 cup finely diced carrot
2 tablespoons finely
    chopped parsley
1/4 teaspoon salt
1/2 teaspoon white pepper

FOR THE SALMON
AND CRAB

1 to 2 tablespoons canola oil
4 (6-ounce) portions wild-caught
    Alaskan King Salmon
1/2 pound crabmeat
24 asparagus spears, peeled,
    blanched, and cut
    into 3-inch lengths
1/2 teaspoon salt
1/2 teaspoon white pepper
Microgreens and orange zest for
    garnish

WILD ALASKAN
KING SALMON OSCAR
with Lump Crab, Sauce Maltaise, Roasted Asparagus, and Quinoa Pilaf

The classic "Oscar" is updated with fresh salmon and topped with tender spring asparagus, delicate crab, and a creamy orange-infused Sauce Maltaise. The dish is accompanied by quinoa, a grain-like seed with a nutty flavor and slightly crunchy texture that is considered a complete protein due to its ideal amino acid balance.

To prepare the sauce: combine the garlic and shallot in a small saucepan with the vinegar, wine, and orange juice; cook over medium-high heat until the mixture reduces to 1/4 cup. Strain the mixture and cool to room temperature. Add the egg yolks to the reduction, pour into the upper pot of a double boiler, and set over simmering water, whisking constantly, until the yolks are cooked and the mixture is fluffy. Remove from the double boiler and use a hand-held blender or whisk to emulsify the mixture while slowly adding the butter in a small stream until fully incorporated; the mixture should be thick and creamy. Season with salt, transfer to a fresh container, and keep warm (about 90 degrees).

To prepare the quinoa: heat the water and salt in a saucepan over medium heat. Add the quinoa to the warm water and bring to a simmer. Cover, reduce the heat, and simmer for approximately 13 minutes, or until cooked but still firm to the bite. Strain, cool, and set aside.

To prepare the vegetables: melt the butter over medium heat in a separate sauté pan until the foam subsides. Add all the vegetables and sweat on medium heat until tender, about 15 minutes. Add the drained quinoa to the pan and mix thoroughly; add parsley, salt, and pepper. Set aside and keep warm.

To prepare the salmon and crab: coat a large sauté pan with the oil and heat over medium-high heat. Working in batches, sear the salmon until golden and crisp; turn it over and sear the other side, not quite as crisp. Set aside the cooked salmon on a baking sheet until all batches are seared; tent with foil to keep warm. Add the crab and asparagus to the hot sauté pan, season with salt and pepper and cook over medium-high heat for about 6 minutes. Remove from heat.

To serve the entrée: spoon some of the quinoa in the center of the plate and top with a piece of salmon. Arrange asparagus spears on top of the salmon and spoon some of the crab mixture over the asparagus. Finish the plate by pouring some of the sauce over the top; garnish with microgreens and orange zest.

Wine Pairing Bodega Naiades, Verdejo, Rueda, Spain

Tasting Notes Lots of richness here, with a bit of citrus influence and some lightness blended in with the quinoa pilaf. This dish really wants dry, crisp, and pure wine with some great acidity to balance out all the flavors.

MAKES 6 SERVINGS

FOR THE RIB-EYES

2 cups canola oil

5 cloves garlic, halved

1 shallot, peeled and cut into
     1/2-inch slices

1 lemon, zest only

2 sprigs fresh thyme

2 sprigs fresh rosemary

1 tablespoon brown sugar

6 (12-ounce) bison rib-eye
     steaks, trimmed

FOR THE RAGOUT

1/4 cup canola oil

1 large white onion, julienned

1 clove garlic, peeled and minced

1/2 cup white wine

2 cups packed oyster mushrooms
     (fans only)

1 cup veal stock

1/2 teaspoon salt

1/4 teaspoon ground
     white pepper

2 sprigs thyme

LEMON- AND HERB-MARINATED BUFFALO RIB-EYE
with Oyster Mushroom Ragout and Red Flannel Hash

Buffalo is a popular offering at the Wild Sage, and although the rib-eye has less fat than its beef counterpart, the steak is tender and full of prime rib flavor. Buffalo steaks can be cooked to the same doneness as beef; rare to medium will ensure the best taste. Here the steak is paired with a potato and root vegetable hash, topped with a rich ragout sauce made from oyster mushrooms.

FOR THE HASH

1 sweet potato, peeled and diced
     (1/4-inch cubes)

1 parsnip, peeled and diced
     (1/4-inch cubes)

1 carrot, peeled and diced
     (1/4-inch cubes)

1 red beet, peeled and diced
     (1/4-inch cubes)

1 celery root, peeled and diced
     (1/4-inch cubes)

1 Yukon Gold potato, peeled and
     diced (1/4-inch cubes)

6 tablespoons butter

2 cloves garlic, brunoised

1 shallot, peeled and minced

4 strips bacon, julienned, cooked,
     and drained

2 teaspoons lemon thyme
     (leaves only)

To prepare the rib-eyes: combine all ingredients except the steaks in a large mixing bowl. Toss steaks in the marinade and coat all surfaces evenly. Put the steaks and marinade in a nonreactive container and store overnight in the marinade, turning several times.

To prepare the ragout: heat the oil in a medium-size sauté pan over low heat. Cook the onion, stirring occasionally, until caramelized. Add the garlic and cook for 2 minutes, then deglaze with the white wine. Add mushrooms and veal stock, and reduce by one-fifth. Season with salt and pepper, and steep the thyme in the mixture for 2 minutes. Remove pan from the heat; remove thyme and discard.

To prepare the hash: cook each vegetable separately in a large saucepan until tender, then shock in ice water.

Once cool remove vegetables from ice bath and drain completely. Heat butter in a sauté pan and cook garlic and shallot until translucent but not browned. Add the vegetables and bacon; cook until heated through. Add the thyme and remove from heat; set aside and keep warm.

To serve the entrée: preheat the grill. Drain off all excess marinade from the steaks. Grill the rib-eyes to desired temperature. Spoon some of the hash in the center of each plate and top with a steak. Spoon some of the ragout over the top.

Wine Pairing Spring Mountain Syrah, Napa, California

Tasting Notes The syrah complements the gamey, zesty, earthy, rich flavors of this dish.

MAKES 4–5 SERVINGS

FOR THE BROTH

4 whole kaffir lime leaves

2 stalks lemongrass, brunoised

4 cloves garlic, peeled and chopped

1 thumb-size ginger lobe, peeled
    and minced

1 shallot, peeled and sliced

2 cups veal stock

2 tablespoons soy sauce

FOR THE RISOTTO

5 tablespoons butter, divided

1/2 cup shiitake mushrooms

1 tablespoon olive oil

1/2 cup diced white onion

9 ounces Carnaroli rice

1 cup white wine

4 cups chicken broth

2 ounces Grana Padano cheese,
    grated

Salt and pepper to taste

FOR THE SALAD

1/3 cup cilantro, stems only

1/2 cup julienned carrots

1/4 cup bean sprouts

OPAL BASIL–STUFFED STATLER CHICKEN BREAST
with Shiitake Mushroom Risotto,
Kaffir Lime and Lemongrass Broth,
and Cilantro Branch Salad

Aromatic opal basil is tucked under the skin of chicken breasts that are pan-fried until golden brown and crispy. Kaffir lime leaf and lemongrass—ingredients used in many Thai recipes—add a punch of refreshing "green" flavor to the complex broth that accompanies the chicken, which is also paired with an earthy mushroom risotto.

FOR THE VINAIGRETTE

2 tablespoons minced
    fresh ginger

1 clove garlic, peeled and minced

2 tablespoons soy sauce

3 tablespoons rice wine vinegar

1 tablespoon brown sugar

1/4 teaspoon fresh lime juice

1/2 cup canola oil

FOR THE CHICKEN

5 Statler chicken breasts, sinew
    removed

5 large whole opal basil leaves

1/2 teaspoon salt

1/2 teaspoon black pepper

2 tablespoons canola oil

To prepare the broth: combine the lime leaves, lemongrass, garlic, ginger, shallot, and stock in a tall-sided saucepan; cook over medium-high heat until reduced to 1 cup. Remove from the heat and let the mixture rest 10 minutes; stir in the soy sauce and strain. Set aside and keep warm.

To prepare the risotto: heat 1 tablespoon of the butter in a medium sauté pan over medium heat. Add the mushrooms and sauté until lightly browned; set aside. Heat the oil in a large saucepan over medium heat. Add the onion and sauté until translucent. Add the rice and increase the heat to medium-high; cook for 1 minute until rice is translucent. Deglaze with the wine and cook until absorbed. Add 1 cup broth at a time, cooking and stirring until all liquid is absorbed. The mixture should be creamy, and the rice should be tender but slightly firm. Remove from heat and fold in cheese, mushrooms, the remaining 4 tablespoons butter, salt, and pepper. Set aside and keep warm.

To prepare the salad: toss all the ingredients together and chill.

To prepare the vinaigrette: combine all the ingredients except the oil in a blender or food processor, and blend until smooth; slowly add the oil until it emulsifies into the mixture. Strain and set aside in the refrigerator.

To prepare the chicken: gently pull the skin up from the breast on one side. Place one basil leaf under the skin of each breast and carefully replace the skin. Season the non-skin side with salt and pepper. Heat the oven to 400 degrees F. In a large sauté pan, heat the oil over medium-high. Sear the chicken breasts skin-side-down until the fat is rendered and the breasts are golden brown. Turn over and sear the meat side for 2 minutes. Remove from the

pan, arrange on a baking sheet and finish in the oven for 6 minutes. Remove the chicken, debone it, and cut into 1/2-inch slices.

To serve the entrée: spoon some of the risotto in the center of each large soup bowl. Arrange the sliced and fanned chicken breast on top of the risotto. Toss the salad in the vinaigrette and place on top of the breast. Drizzle the broth around the risotto.

Wine Pairing **Domaine Weinbach "Cuvee St. Catherine" Riesling, Alsace, France**

Tasting Notes **An Alsatian Riesling pairs well with the exotic Thai-influenced dish that has prevalent flavors of lime, basil, and lemongrass.**

MAKES 5–6 SERVINGS

FOR THE CAKE

3 eggs

1 cup sugar

1 tablespoon finely chopped
   lemon zest

1 tablespoon finely chopped
   orange zest

1 teaspoon finely chopped lime zest

3/4 cup olive oil

1/4 cup milk

1-1/2 cups sifted flour

2/3 cup finely ground pistachios

1/2 teaspoon salt

2 teaspoons baking powder

FOR THE STRAWBERRIES

1 pint strawberries, washed, hulled,
   and quartered

1/2 cup sugar

Pinch of salt

1 tablespoon white balsamic
   vinegar

2 tablespoons premium vodka (such
   as Grey Goose brand)

FOR THE COULIS

1 cup strawberries, picked and
   cleaned

1 cup water

1 cup sugar

CITRUS-PISTACHIO OLIVE OIL CAKE
with Vodka Balsamic Strawberries and Vanilla Crema

This sophisticated version of strawberry shortcake pairs a light cake made with finely ground pistachios, a sweet custard-based sauce, and fresh berries spiked with vodka. A surprise dash of aged balsamic vinegar brings out the berries' red color and enhances their sweet flavor.

FOR THE CRÈME ANGLAISE

1 cup heavy cream

1 vanilla bean, split and scraped

Pinch of salt

3 egg yolks

1/4 cup sugar

FOR THE CREMA

1 cup heavy cream

1 vanilla bean

1/4 cup powdered sugar

FOR THE GARNISH

6 fresh mint sprigs

To prepare the cake: preheat the oven to 325 degrees F.
Using the whisk attachment of an electric mixer, combine
the eggs and sugar in a metal bowl and process until the
mixture is pale yellow. Add the zests, oil, and milk, and
combine. Transfer mixture to a large mixing bowl and
fold in the remaining ingredients by hand, just until combined; do not overmix. Line a 10 x 10-inch baking pan
with parchment paper and spray with nonstick cooking
spray. Pour the batter in the pan evenly and bake for 35
minutes, or until a toothpick inserted in the cake comes
out clean. Move the cake to a wire rack and cool to
room temperature.

To prepare the strawberries: place them in a medium-
size bowl. Sprinkle with sugar and salt, and stir gently.
Let rest for 15 minutes. Drizzle vinegar and vodka over
the strawberries. Gently stir one more time. Refrigerate
until serving time.

To prepare the coulis: combine all the ingredients in a
tall-sided, heavy-bottomed saucepan and heat over
medium heat until the mixture simmers. Continue simmering until the mixture is reduced by half and small
syrupy bubbles form. Transfer the mixture to a blender
and purée. Strain the coulis through a fine mesh sieve
and cool in the refrigerator.

To prepare the crème anglaise: scald the cream with the
vanilla bean and salt. In a metal mixing bowl, cream
together the yolks and sugar until light yellow. Add cream
and temper the yolks. Make a double boiler and cook
mixture, constantly stirring, until it reaches 175 degrees
and coats the back of a spoon; strain and chill.

To prepare the crema: in an electric mixer with the whisk
attachment, process the heavy cream at high speed. Once
it begins to increase in volume, split the vanilla bean and
scrape the seeds into the bowl; add the sugar. Continue to
process at high speed until the mixture is light and fluffy,
and holds its shape, about 3–4 minutes.

To serve the dessert: using a 4-inch circular cookie cutter,
cut rounds out of the cake. Place a round on each plate
and top with the strawberries and some of the juice.
Spoon on some of the crema, followed by the coulis
and crème anglaise; garnish with mint sprigs.

MAKES 6 SERVINGS

FOR THE PANNA COTTA

4 cups cold water
5-1/2 gelatin sheets
10 ounces coconut milk
1-1/4 cups heavy cream
1 lime, zest only
1 orange, zest only
1 lemon, zest only
1/2 cup sugar

FOR THE COOKIE

9 tablespoons butter
1-1/3 cups powdered sugar
4 egg whites
1 cup flour
Pinch of salt
1 tablespoon poppy seeds

FOR THE ICE

1 cup hulled, sliced strawberries
1 cup water
1 tablespoon rose water
1 cup sugar
1 cup water

FOR THE GARNISH

1 kiwi, peeled and cut into 6 slices
3 strawberries, cleaned and sliced

CITRUS AND COCONUT PANNA COTTA
with Strawberry–Rose Petal Ice and Poppy Seed Cookie

Panna cotta, literally "cooked cream" in Italian, is a cool pudding-like dessert that gets a tropical flavor from the addition of coconut milk and the zest of lemon, lime, and orange. Old-fashioned rose water adds a soft garden taste and scent to a refreshing strawberry ice, and the dessert is accompanied by a crispy poppy seed cookie.

To prepare the panna cotta: place the cold water and gelatin in a suitable-size container and bloom for 15 minutes. In a tall-sided saucepan, add all the remaining ingredients and bring to a low boil. Remove the gelatin sheets from the water and squeeze out all excess moisture. Add gelatin sheets to the cream mixture, stir to dissolve, and remove from the heat. Strain the mixture through a fine mesh sieve and pour into 6 small martini glasses. Chill in the glasses for 4 hours or overnight to set the gelatin.

To prepare the cookie: cream the butter with the sugar. Add egg whites and scrape down the sides; mix for 1 minute. Combine the flour and salt, and slowly add to butter mixture until a dough forms. Chill dough 10 minutes in the refrigerator. Add poppy seeds and then fill disposable pastry bag with batter. Preheat oven to 350 degrees F. Pipe 30 (3 x 1/2-inch) cigar shapes onto a parchment-lined sheet pan. Bake for 8 minutes, turning once.

To prepare the ice: bring all ingredients to a simmer in a saucepan and gently cook for 4 minutes. Remove mixture from the heat and strain into a small shallow container. Place the mixture in the freezer. After the first hour, remove from the freezer, scrape the ice with a fork, and return to the freezer. Repeat this process for the next 3 hours, until completely frozen. The end product should be small frozen shards.

To serve the dessert: place 1 slice of kiwi in the center of the panna cotta in the martini glasses. Scrape the ice once more and place a small nest on top of the kiwi. Garnish with a strawberry slice and cookie.

MAKES 8 SERVINGS

FOR THE CAKE

1/2 pound (2 sticks) butter
8 ounces dark chocolate, finely
    chopped
2 tablespoons Baileys Irish Cream
2 tablespoons Kahlúa
2 tablespoons Grand Marnier
4 eggs
1/4 cup sugar

FOR THE COULIS

1 vanilla bean, split
1 cup raspberries
1 cup water
1 cup sugar

FOR THE CRÈME ANGLAISE

1 vanilla bean, split
1 cup heavy cream
Pinch of salt
3 egg yolks
1/4 cup sugar

FOR THE GARNISH

Whipped cream
Chocolate cigarettes
Mint sprigs

CHOCOLATE TRUFFLE CAKE
with Raspberry-Vanilla Coulis

This dense chocolate cake—like its namesake, the wildly alcoholic B-52 shot—is flavored with Kahlúa, Baileys Irish Cream, and Grand Marnier liqueurs. A light custard swirled with fresh raspberry sauce offsets the rich, intensely chocolate flavor of the cake.

To prepare the cake: preheat the oven to 300 degrees F. Lightly spray an 8-inch square baking dish with nonstick spray and then line with parchment paper. Set up a double boiler with a metal mixing bowl. In the double boiler, melt the butter with the chocolate and liqueurs. In a separate bowl, mix the eggs with the sugar until pale yellow. Emulsify the chocolate mixture into the egg and sugar mixture. Spoon the batter into the prepared baking dish and bake for 45 minutes, or until set. Let cool completely, then cover and chill overnight in the refrigerator. Remove from pan.

To prepare the coulis: scrape the seeds from the vanilla bean; combine the seeds and the remaining ingredients in a tall-sided saucepan; simmer over medium heat until mixture is reduced by half. Small syrupy bubbles will start to form. Transfer mixture to a blender and purée. Strain mixture through a fine mesh sieve and cool in the refrigerator.

To prepare the crème anglaise: scrape the seeds from the vanilla bean; combine the seeds with the cream and salt in a medium saucepan. Heat the mixture over medium-high heat to scald the cream; remove from the heat before it boils. In a metal mixing bowl, cream together the yolks and sugar until light yellow. Add the cream mixture and temper the yolks. Make a double boiler and cook mixture, constantly stirring, until it reaches 175 degrees and coats the back of a spoon. Strain mixture through a fine mesh sieve and cool in the refrigerator.

To serve the dessert: remove the cake from the pan and use a 2-inch round cutter to cut 8 pieces of cake; place one cake on each plate. Pour a ring of crème anglaise around the cake and fill the center with the coulis. Drag a wooden skewer through the two sauces to create a sunburst effect. Use two spoons to dollop the whipped cream in a quenelle shape and place on top of the cake; garnish with a chocolate cigarette and mint sprigs.

SUMMER INVITES

Do I Want to Plant a Garden?

Do I want to plant a garden?

Well, gosh Almighty, Yes!

After six good months of winter

I'd think you'd orter guess

A man's most awful hungry

For a mess o' garden truck;

Fer spinach, peas, an' onions

An' all that sort of chuck

To feel my teeth a crunchin'

On some tender juicy greens,

For a six-weeks-ole sweet turnip

I'd give my Sunday jeans!

Maude Wenonah Willford, 1930

NATIVE AMERICANS had excellent taste when it came to choosing a summer home. For hundreds of years before trappers and homesteaders arrived in Jackson Hole, tribes came to the valley during warm summer months to harvest the abundant fish and game. The area's moderate temperatures, rich valley grasses, and numerous lakes and streams provided a comfortable summer retreat. Today, Jackson Hole remains a popular location for summer homes and tourist visits—summer is the area's busiest season. As a gateway city to Yellowstone, Jackson hosts an estimated three million visitors each summer as they pass through on their way to the country's most famous national park.

Like winter visitors, Jackson Hole's summer guests are drawn to the area's unrivaled scenery and wide range of recreational opportunities: hiking, biking, fishing, rafting, golfing, picnicking, kayaking, horseback riding—or even just sitting on the deck to admire the glorious views. With the short summer season—snow can fall as late as June and as early as August—the goal is to pack as much in a day as possible.

From May to September, hikers discover a visual treat with the colorful wildflowers that carpet the valley and alpine meadows. Skyrocket gilia, larkspur, Indian paintbrush, and lupine bloom in the valley as temperatures rise. Fireweed, columbine, monkshood, and the rare calypso orchid enjoy the moist environment of the forest floor. Alpine zone plants with very small flowers grow close to the ground and include moss campion, alpine forget-me-not, sky, pilot, and arnica—a plant prized for centuries for its healing properties (see page 64).

In town during the summer months, visitors feel transported back in time as Jackson vibrates with sounds from the past: the jingle of harnesses and the whinny of horses as the stagecoach offers rides around the Town Square, the rattle of shoes and boots on the wooden sidewalks as customers wander in and out of the town's charming shops, and the deafening roar of gunfire during the 6:00 p.m. nightly staged gunfight by the famous Shoot Out gang.

One highly anticipated summer event on the Fourth of July is Music in the Hole, a free outdoor community concert featuring the Grand Teton Music Festival Orchestra. Rusty Parrot owner Ron Harrison worked with music director Eiji Oue to create this event in 1997, and it has become a Jackson Hole tradition. Spectators arrive early with picnics and blankets to get front row seats on the field, visiting with neighbors and catching up on local news until the performance begins. The rousing concert is followed by a spectacular fireworks display over Snow King Mountain.

Another favorite summer event is the Jackson Farmers Market. With a short growing season—only 60 frost-free days a year—the Jackson area is a high-country gardening challenge. Gardeners and farmers bring the fruits (or vegetables) of their labor to the farmers market on the Town Square each Saturday from July through September. Vendors sell their fresh produce, baked goods, organic meats, fresh cut flowers, live potted plants, sauces, and much more.

A new menu marks the arrival of summertime at the Wild Sage, and the kitchen takes full advantage of the fleeting abundance of seasonal fruits and vegetables. Cool soups and gazpachos offer a welcome respite from balmy days, and salads are rich with garden-fresh produce like heirloom tomatoes and tender lettuces tossed in light, house-made salad dressings.

Unusual offerings from the fish market arrive daily throughout the summer, and diners may be pleasantly surprised to find rarities such as day-boat scallops and soft-shell crabs on the menu. House-made ice creams and sorbets are the perfect ending to a summertime meal, but there's always the temptation to splurge on a chocolate dessert like rich cheesecake or the kitchen's trademark crispy beignets dusted with cinnamon sugar.

The Cultural Side of Summer: Grand Teton Music Festival and Jackson Hole Center for the Arts

Since 1962, Jackson's hills come alive with the sound of music each summer as the Grand Teton Music Festival takes the stage at Walk Festival Hall in Teton Village. Regarded as one of the countries most important summer music festivals, the Jackson Hole event has welcomed some of the world's most celebrated artists to its Walk Festival Hall, and the Grand Teton Music Festival's all-wooden performance facility is acclaimed by listeners and performers alike for its superb acoustics and intimate atmosphere. For a schedule of performances, visit their website at www.gtmf.org.

In the town of Jackson, the Center for the Arts provides an architecturally elegant venue for the resident year-round theater troupe Off Square Theatre Company, as well as attracting nationally known artists from every aspect of the arts. The Center for the Arts campus consists of the 41,000-square-foot Arts & Education Pavilion as well as the recently completed Performing Arts Pavilion that includes a 500-seat theater. For a schedule of upcoming performances, visit their website at www.jhcenterforthearts.org.

Indigenous Ingredients: Arnica at The Body Sage

For centuries, arnica has been used in herbal medicine to treat bruises, sprains, and stiff muscles. The flowering mountain plant, a member of the sunflower family, contains

sesquiterpene lactones, substances known to reduce inflammation and decrease pain.

Intrigued by the indigenous plant's healing properties, especially for sore muscles, Heidi Harrison, founder of the Rusty Parrot's in-house Body Sage spa, uses arnica from local alpine meadows to create her popular Sports Recovery Package. The package includes a sports massage, herbal wrap, and salt glow—guaranteed to soothe the weary muscles of the Rusty Parrot Lodge's active guests.

Opened in 1995, The Body Sage was the first spa in Jackson, earning it the "local's favorite" moniker. Today the spa continues to provide guests with pampering and various spa therapy options to complement the area's outdoor lifestyle, including many organic and indigenous herbs and treatments.

MAKES 6 SERVINGS

FOR THE BROTH

4 cups orange juice (preferably freshly squeezed Valencia orange juice)

1/4 cup sugar

1 vanilla bean, scraped

2 large ginger lobes, peeled and chopped (about 1/2 cup)

1 stalk lemongrass, bruised and cut into 1-inch pieces

2 kaffir lime leaves

FOR THE SOUP

1 mango, peeled, seeded, and cut into 1/2-inch pieces

1 papaya, peeled, seeded, and cut into 1/2-inch pieces

2 kiwis, peeled and cut into 1/2-inch pieces

12 blackberries

12 raspberries

2 ounces vanilla grass

2 tablespoons packed fresh mint chiffonade

FRUIT SOUP
with Spicy Ginger and Orange Broth, and Vanilla Grass

Cool and fresh, this jewel-toned summer soup is a perfect light starter that gets an extra burst of flavor from fresh ginger and lemongrass.

For the broth: combine all of the broth ingredients in a tall saucepan and cook over medium heat until the mixture simmers. Simmer for 10 minutes, remove from the heat, and strain the mixture through a fine mesh sieve. Cool in the refrigerator until completely chilled.

To serve the soup: ladle the broth into six chilled bowls and divide the fresh fruit among the bowls. Garnish with vanilla grass and mint.

MAKES 4 TO 6 SERVINGS

FOR THE OIL

1 cup canola oil

2 ounces chives, chopped
(1/2-inch pieces)

FOR THE SOUP

2 tablespoons canola oil

3 leeks (white part only), cleaned
and cut (enough for 2 packed
cups)

4 cloves garlic, sliced

2 cups peeled and diced (large
chunks) cassava root

6 cups chicken stock

1 teaspoon salt

1/8 teaspoon freshly ground white
pepper

2 cups heavy cream

FOR THE CRACKLINGS

3 pieces bacon lardons

CASSAVA AND LEEK POTAGE
with Chive Oil and Bacon Lardons

Cassava is also known as yuca, a starchy root vegetable often used in Latin and Caribbean cuisine. Here it is cooked with leeks and garlic to make the base for a creamy soup that is topped with crispy bacon crumbles and a drizzle of bright green chive-infused oil.

To prepare the chive oil: one day before, process the oil and chives in a blender for 30 seconds. Put mixture into an airtight container and refrigerate for 24 hours. Strain through a fine chinois and let drain for 1 hour. Do not push any solids through; set aside.

To prepare the soup: heat a large saucepan over medium-high heat and add canola oil, leeks, and garlic. Cook for several minutes, or until the leeks are translucent. Add cassava and stock, and let simmer for 20 to 25 minutes. Season with salt and pepper, add the heavy cream, and purée in a blender.

To prepare the cracklings: place bacon lardons in a cold pan and render over medium heat for 12 minutes, constantly turning. Drain off the excess fat, set cracklings aside, and keep warm.

To serve the soup: ladle into bowls and top with the cracklings.

SUMMER SALADS

FOR THE VINAIGRETTE

1 tablespoon dried hibiscus flowers
1/4 cup white balsamic vinegar
2 strawberries, quartered
1 tablespoon sugar
1/4 teaspoon salt
1/2 cup oil

FOR THE PRALINE

1 cup whole pecans
1 cup warm water
1/4 cup powdered sugar
1/8 teaspoon salt

FOR THE FENNEL

1 cup water
1 cup sugar
1 fennel bulb, sliced paper thin

FOR THE SALAD

1-1/2 pounds assorted organic baby
    lettuces or mixed lettuces

FOR THE GARNISH

12 fresh strawberries, tops
    removed, cut into quarters

ORGANIC BABY LETTUCES,
Strawberry-Hibiscus Vinaigrette,
Pecan Praline, and Candied Fennel

Tender baby greens are tossed in a strawberry-based vinaigrette that gets its ruby red color from the addition of dried, vitamin C-rich hibiscus flowers. Candied pecans and paper-thin fennel bulb slices are tossed with the salad to add crunch and provide sweetness to balance the white balsamic vinegar in the dressing.

To prepare the vinaigrette: let the hibiscus hydrate in the vinegar for 20 minutes. Strain through a fine mesh sieve and squeeze juice out of flower petals. Add strawberries, sugar, and salt to vinegar mixture and process. Slowly emulsify oil into mixture and then strain through a fine mesh sieve.

To prepare the praline: add pecans to warm water and soak for 1 minute. Drain completely and then toss in powdered sugar mixed with salt. Bake at 300 degrees F for 40 minutes, turning periodically. Let air-dry on a baking sheet.

To prepare the fennel: bring the water and sugar to a simmer in a tall-sided saucepan. Add the fennel and cook for 10 minutes. Let stand in mixture 1 hour. Drain and place on a baking sheet to dry and crisp.

To serve the salad: toss the lettuces with the vinaigrette and distribute among chilled salad plates. Garnish each plate with 2 quartered strawberries, a scatter of pralines, and candied fennel.

MAKES 6 SERVINGS

FOR THE OIL

2 cups lightly packed fresh basil
   leaves
1/2 cup loosely packed parsley
1 cup canola oil
1 tablespoon white truffle oil

FOR THE SYRUP

1 cup balsamic vinegar
1 cup ruby port wine
1 shallot, peeled and halved
1 clove garlic, peeled and halved

FOR THE SALAD

2 green zebra-stripe tomatoes,
   cut in 1/2-inch slices
2 purple Cherokee tomatoes,
   cut in 1/2-inch slices
2 sunburst tomatoes, cut in
   1/2-inch slices
3/4 pound extra-firm tofu, cut in
   1/4-inch slices
1/2 teaspoon kosher salt
1 avocado, peeled and pitted
1 cup opal basil leaves, loosely
   packed
1/2 cup orange mint leaves

FOR THE GARNISH

1/8 cup basil leaves, chiffonade
1/8 cup orange mint leaves,
   chiffonade

HEIRLOOM TOMATOES
with Organic Tofu, Avocado, Port-Balsamic Syrup, and Basil-Infused Truffle Oil

This composed salad celebrates the summer garden with heirloom tomatoes, stacked fresh herbs, and mild slices of tofu. A deconstructed dressing pairs a slow-cooked, balsamic vinegar syrup with a bright green oil infused with basil and parsley.

To prepare the oil: process the basil, parsley, and oils for 30 seconds in a food processor fitted with a metal blade. Put all contents into an airtight container and refrigerate for 24–36 hours. Strain through a fine chinois and let drain for 1 hour. Do not push any solids through. Set aside in the refrigerator to chill.

To prepare the syrup: combine all the ingredients in a small saucepan over medium heat and cook at a very low simmer until slightly reduced. After 10 minutes, remove the shallot and garlic. Continue cooking until the mixture forms small syrupy bubbles, gains viscosity, and is reduced by 80 percent. (Note: This reduction has to be cooked very slowly—never at a boil—or it will become bitter.)

To prepare and serve the salad: on a clean work surface, lay out all the tomato and tofu slices, and season with salt and a light drizzle of basil-truffle oil. Layer tomato, tofu, and herbs in an alternating fashion.

Cut the avocado into 6 wedges, cut each wedge into a fan. Top the tomato-tofu stacks with the avocado fan and garnish with the herb chiffonades. Drizzle more basil-truffle oil and balsamic syrup around the stack.

MAKES 6 SERVINGS

FOR THE SAUCE

1/2 cup corn syrup
1/2 teaspoon lime juice
1/2 teaspoon lemon juice
1/2 teaspoon yuzu
1/2 teaspoon rice wine vinegar
3 tablespoons soy sauce

FOR THE VINAIGRETTE

2 tablespoons peeled and minced
    fresh ginger
1 clove garlic, peeled and minced
2 tablespoons soy sauce
3 tablespoons rice wine vinegar
1 tablespoon brown sugar
1/4 teaspoon fresh lime juice
1/2 cup canola oil

FOR THE CASHEWS

1 cup raw cashews
1 cup warm water
2 tablespoons powdered sugar
1/4 teaspoon cayenne pepper
1/8 teaspoon salt

FOR THE PURÉE

1/2 teaspoon wasabi powder
1/2 cup shelled and blanched
    edamame
1/2 cup water
1-1/2 teaspoons grapeseed oil

YAKINORI SALAD ROLL
with Wasabi-Edamame Purée, Opal Basil, Spicy Cashews, and Citrus Ponzu Sauce

Salad greens are rolled inside a wrapper of yakinori—toasted seaweed—in this sushi-inspired preparation. The rolls are served with an assortment of sauces for dipping and topped with a sprinkling of crunchy cashews.

FOR THE SALAD ROLL

4 tablespoons opal basil leaf
    chiffonade (about 15 leaves)
3 tablespoons mint leaf chiffon-
    ade (about 40 leaves)
3 cups Napa cabbage julienne
    (about 1 head)
6 sheets nori
1 carrot, peeled and julienned
1/4 pound fresh bean sprouts
1/4 cup cold water

FOR THE GARNISH

Daikon sprouts
Sriracha
Kecap manis

To prepare the sauce: combine all the ingredients in a mixing bowl using a wire whisk. Set aside in the refrigerator.

To prepare the vinaigrette: process the ginger, garlic, soy, vinegar, brown sugar, and lime juice in a blender. Slowly drizzle the oil into the mixture with the blender running until oil is fully emulsified. Strain through a chinois, discard any solids, and set aside in the refrigerator to chill.

To prepare the cashews: preheat oven to 290 degrees F. Add raw nuts to water and soak for 1 minute, then strain. Combine the powdered sugar, cayenne pepper, and salt in a small bowl, and toss the cashews in the mixture. Spread the nuts on a baking sheet and bake for 40 minutes, turning periodically. Remove from the oven and cool on the baking sheet.

To prepare the purée: combine the wasabi powder, edamame, and water in a blender and process until smooth. Slowly drizzle the oil into the mixture with the blender running until oil is fully emulsified. Set aside in the refrigerator and chill.

To prepare the salad roll: combine the basil, mint, and cabbage in a large mixing bowl. Lay out a bamboo sushi matt and place a sheet of nori in the center. Place 1/6 of the cabbage mixture horizontally in the center of the sheet. Place carrot and bean sprouts on top of the cabbage and roll into a cylinder using the matt. Seal the roll with dabs of cold water on the farthest end. Set aside and proceed with the remaining sheets, using the same procedure.

To serve the salad roll: using a sharp knife, slice the salad rolls into eight equal portions. Arrange the slices cut-side-up in a straight line down the center of the plate, eight pieces per plate. Drizzle vinaigrette over each roll and top with the cashews and daikon sprouts. Place sriracha, kecap manis, and wasabi-edamame purée on the plate alongside the roll. Portion the ponzu sauce in small bowls for dipping.

MAKES 4–5 SERVINGS

FOR THE CARROTS

2 large carrots
Canola oil for frying

For the beurre blanc:
1/2 pound (2 sticks) butter
2 tablespoons fresh lime juice
1 cup white wine
1 tablespoon peeled and minced
    shallots
1 bay leaf
1 clove garlic, peeled and minced

FOR THE SCALLOPS

Canola oil
15 day-boat scallops (8-10 per-
    pound count)
1 teaspoon salt
1 teaspoon freshly ground black
    pepper
1 pound baby spinach
1/4 pound bacon, cut in 1/2-inch
    pieces and cooked until crispy

PAN-SEARED DAY-BOAT SCALLOPS
with Spinach Salad, Citrus Beurre Blanc, and Crispy Carrots

This light summer appetizer pairs lightly caramelized sea scallops topped with tender sautéed spinach, crispy bacon, flash-fried carrots, and a classic, creamy beurre blanc sauce.

To prepare the carrots: peel the carrots and cut them very fine on a rotating slicer (the Wild Sage chef uses a Japanese-style slicer) or mandoline. Heat the oil in a deep fryer or in a heavy saucepan over medium-high heat until it reaches 320 degrees F. Cook the carrots until they stop bubbling and are lightly crisp. Drain on a tray lined with paper towels and let air-dry in a single layer for at least 1 hour.

To prepare the beurre blanc: cut the butter into 1-inch cubes; chill. Combine the remaining ingredients in a medium saucepan and heat over medium heat. Simmer until the mixture is reduced by 85 percent. Using a whisk, add one cube of butter at a time until all are incorporated. Strain and keep warm.

To prepare the scallops: brush a medium-size sauté pan with oil and heat over medium-high heat. Season the scallops with salt and pepper, and sear them in the hot pan until golden brown, about 3 minutes; turn and sear the other side. Drain excess oil and use the same pan to quickly cook the spinach with the bacon until the mixture begins to get lightly crispy.

To serve the appetizer: divide the spinach and bacon between 4 or 5 plates and spoon the mixture in the middle of each. Arrange the scallops on top of the spinach, drizzle with beurre blanc, and garnish with carrots.

Wine Pairing Villa Maria Clifford Bay Sauvignon Blanc, Marlborough, Awatere Valley, New Zealand

Tasting Notes Crisp, dry, lots of citrus on the nose, great acidity, and extremely refreshing.

MAKES 6 SERVINGS

FOR THE BISCUITS

2 small sweet potatoes
2 bacon slices
1/2 cup flour
2-1/4 teaspoons baking powder
1/4 teaspoon salt
1 tablespoon sugar

FOR THE AIOLI

1 chayote, peeled
1-1/2 teaspoons canola oil
1/8 teaspoon salt
1/8 teaspoon black pepper
2 egg yolks
2 cloves garlic, peeled and roasted
1 tablespoon lemon juice
1 cup canola oil
Pinch of salt
2 tablespoons finely sliced fresh
    chives

FOR THE CONFITURE

1/2 cup sugar
1/2 cup water
1/2 lemon, juiced
1/2 cup peeled and diced fresh
    horseradish (large chunks)
5 Roma tomatoes

CHESAPEAKE BAY SOFT-SHELL CRAB BLT
with Cracklin' Sweet Potato Biscuit, Lemon and Chive Aioli, Watercress, and Tomato Confiture

This Southern-inspired starter has all the elements of a BLT—but with a lot more imagination! Seasonal soft-shell crabs are pan-fried and layered with tender sweet potato biscuits, a fresh tomato "jam," homemade mayonnaise, and baby watercress.

FOR THE CRAB

1 cup flour
1 tablespoon Old Bay seasoning
1/4 teaspoon freshly ground black
    pepper
6 tablespoons canola oil
6 prime soft-shell crabs, cleaned

FOR THE GARNISH

Micro watercress

To prepare the biscuits: preheat the oven to 350 degrees F. Roast the sweet potatoes for approximately 45 minutes, until cooked through. Remove and discard the skin from the potatoes; mash, reserving 1 cup (any remaining mashed potato can be used at another time), and keep warm. Slice the bacon into a fine julienne and then fry in a hot sauté pan until crisp. Remove the bacon to a baking sheet lined with paper towels; reserve the bacon fat. Sift together the flour, baking powder, and salt. Add the sugar and bacon fat to the mashed sweet potatoes and combine; add the dry ingredients and combine; knead for 2 minutes. Roll the dough to 3/4-inch thickness. Cut into circles with a 4-inch round cookie cutter. Raise oven temperature to 425 degrees F and bake for 12–15 minutes.

To prepare the aioli: preheat the grill and slice the chayote into 1/8-inch-thick pieces; brush with oil and sprinkle with salt and pepper. Grill for 1 minute on each side; remove and cool to room temperature, then cut brunoise and set aside.

Blend the egg yolks, garlic, and lemon juice in a food processor. While running slowly, add 1 cup oil in a slow stream until it is emulsified. Remove from the food processor and fold in the salt, chives, and chayote; mix thoroughly and refrigerate.

To prepare the confiture: place the sugar, water, lemon juice, and horseradish in a small saucepan. Reduce until it thickens to syrup. In a large saucepan, bring 2 quarts of water to a boil. Add the tomatoes and cook for 30 seconds, shock in an ice bath, and peel the skin. Fillet the tomatoes and discard the seeds. Add the tomatoes to the syrup and cook for 10 minutes until syrup consistency is regained. Discard the horseradish, set aside the "jam," and cool to room temperature.

To prepare the crab: combine the flour, Old Bay seasoning, and pepper in a small bowl. Heat the oil in a large sauté pan. Dredge the crabs in the flour mixture, dusting off the excess. Pan-fry the crabs for about 2 minutes per side to preferred doneness. Drain on a tray lined with paper towels.

To serve the appetizer: place a biscuit in the center of each plate (you may have to trim it down for a flat surface) and top with a layer of the confiture. Place one crab on top of the biscuit. Finish with a dollop of aioli and micro watercress.

Wine Pairing Domaine Vacheron Les Romains Sancerre, Loire Valley, France

Tasting Notes Great mineral and limestone characteristics.

MAKES 6 SERVINGS

FOR THE PANCETTA

6 ounces pancetta,
    cut in 1/8-inch slices
1 ounce sugar

FOR THE VINAIGRETTE

10 juniper berries
1 tablespoon mustard seed
1 tablespoon coriander seed
4 bay leaves
1 cup rice wine vinegar
1/4 cup sugar
2 cloves garlic
2 shallots
1 ginger lobe (about 1 ounce)
1/2 cup lychee syrup
2 tablespoons yuzu juice
1 cup canola oil
1/2 teaspoon salt
8 canned lychee nuts,
    cut into quarters

FOR THE HEARTS OF PALM

1 cup yuzu juice
2 cups water
1 thumb-size ginger lobe, peeled
2 cloves garlic
1 shallot
1 teaspoon salt
1 pound fresh hearts of palm

TOGARASHI-DUSTED SHRIMP
with Yuzu-Poached Hearts of Palm, Candied Pancetta, Lychee Vinaigrette, and Micro Mizuna

A stunning, stacked Asian-influenced appetizer pairs crispy
fried shrimp with tender poached hearts of palm and a
homemade vinaigrette redolent with the spicy-sweet
aromatic flavor of lychee fruit.

FOR THE SHRIMP

1 pound wild-caught Key West
    shrimp (8–12 per-pound count)
2 tablespoons canola oil
2 tablespoons togarashi

TO FINISH AND GARNISH

2 tablespoons butter
Sweet soy sauce
Hot chile garlic sauce
Micro mizuna

To prepare the pancetta: preheat oven to 350 degrees F. Arrange the pancetta flat on a parchment-lined sheet pan, place another layer of parchment on top followed by another tight-fitting sheet pan. Cook for 14 minutes, uncover, and sprinkle sugar on top in a thin layer. Cook for 10 minutes more, or until crisp and rendered.

To prepare the vinaigrette: combine the juniper berries, mustard seed, coriander seed, bay leaves, vinegar, and sugar in a saucepan and cook over medium-high heat until the mixture is reduced by half. Strain and cool the liquid, discarding the solids. Pour the liquid in a blender and add the garlic, shallots, ginger, lychee syrup, and yuzu juice. Process the ingredients for 3 seconds and slowly add the oil until it is fully emulsified. Strain the mixture, season with salt, and add the lychee nuts; set aside.

To prepare the hearts of palm: set up an ice bath for shocking. Put all ingredients into a saucepan except the hearts of palm and bring to a boil. Add the hearts of palm and cook for 5 minutes; turn off the heat, let stand in the liquid for 2 minutes more, and then shock in an ice bath. Drain when chilled and set aside.

To prepare the shrimp: heat a sauté pan over medium-high heat. Sear the shrimp in the oil about 2 minutes on each side. Drain and sprinkle the shrimp on all sides with the togarishi; set aside.

To finish and serve the appetizer: heat the butter in a separate pan and gently warm the hearts of palm; toss them in the vinaigrette, drain, and place in the center of the plate; top with pancetta. Toss the mizuna in the vinaigrette, drain, and garnish the hearts of palm; top with the seared shrimp. Spoon some of the sweet soy sauce and hot chile garlic sauce around the plate.

Spirit Pairing Rihaku Dreamy Clouds Tokubetsu Junmai Sake, Matsue-shi, Shimane Prefecture, Japan

Tasting Notes Instead of wine, Asian-influenced foods are sometimes best paired with a great, creamy, smooth sake.

MAKES 4 SERVINGS

FOR THE PANCAKES

1 egg
1 tablespoon chopped fresh ginger
2 cloves garlic
1 cup buttermilk
1 cup flour
1 teaspoon baking powder
1/2 teaspoon salt
1 scallion, bias-cut very thin
　　(green only)
2 ounces clarified butter, for finish-
　　ing pancakes

FOR THE GLAZE

1/2 cup yuzu juice (not from con-
　　centrate, if possible)
1/2 cup water
1/4 cup sugar
1 tablespoon cold water
1 tablespoon cornstarch

FOR THE HEBI

1-1/2 pounds wild Hawaiian hebi
　　(6-ounce portions), skinned and
　　boned
1 teaspoon salt
1/2 teaspoon freshly
　　ground black pepper
3 tablespoons canola oil

PAN-SEARED WILD HAWAIIAN HEBI
with Yuzu Glaze, Broccolini, and Scallion-Buttermilk Pancakes

Hebi, commonly known as shortbill spearfish, is a mild amber-colored fish that becomes available from Hawaiian fisheries in the summer and autumn. In this preparation, the Wild Sage glazes the fish with yuzu, a Japanese citrus fruit, and serves it with crisp-tender Broccolini and small, scallion-flecked buttermilk pancakes.

FOR THE BROCCOLINI

2 tablespoons canola oil
2 cloves garlic, minced
1/2 tablespoon fresh ginger
　　brunoise
1 shallot, brunoised
2 dried bird chiles, chopped and
　　crushed
5 ounces Broccolini, cut in 4-inch
　　lengths

To prepare the pancakes: process the egg, ginger, garlic, and buttermilk in a blender for 30 seconds. Remove and strain through a fine mesh strainer. In a metal mixing bowl, combine the remaining dry ingredients with the egg and buttermilk mixture. Mix well until combined; chill.

When ready to serve, preheat an electric griddle to 350 degrees F. Season the griddle with the clarified butter and portion the pancakes with a 1/2-ounce ladle. Cook until small bubbles form on the top, about 1 minute; flip the pancakes and finish cooking the remaining side. Keep the pancakes warm by placing them in a single layer on a paper towel–lined cookie sheet in a 200 degree oven.

To prepare the glaze: combine the juice, 1/2 cup of water, and sugar, and bring to a boil. Make a "slurry" with the cold water and cornstarch. Add the slurry to the boiling mixture and return to a boil to thicken. Once the mixture has thickened, remove from the heat, cover, and keep warm.

To prepare the hebi: preheat two large sauté pans, one over high heat and one over medium heat. Season the hebi with salt on both sides and pepper on skin side. Heat the oil over high heat and sear the hebi, non-skin-side first, for about 2 minutes. Turn the fish and cook 2 minutes more. Remove from the pan and let rest for 3 minutes.

To prepare the Broccolini: start the vegetables while the fish is resting. Add the oil to the medium-heat pan and then add the garlic, ginger, shallot, and chiles; sauté for 1 minute but do not brown. Add the Broccolini and cook to al dente.

To serve the entrée: arrange the pancakes and the Broccolini on the plate and top the vegetables with the fish. Spoon some of the warm yuzu glaze over the fish.

Wine Pairing **Prinz von Hessen Riesling Classic, Rheingau, Germany**

Tasting Notes **The classic pancake presentation and citrus/acidity of the yuzu glaze pairs well with a dry German Riesling.**

FOR THE BROTH

2 Ancho chiles
4 Roma tomatoes, roughly chopped
1 cup veal stock
4 cloves garlic, peeled
1 shallot, peeled
1/4 teaspoon salt

FOR THE RELISH

4 Roma tomatoes, seeded and
    diced (1/4-inch cubes)
1 shallot brunoise
1/4 cup Indian pudina (mint) pickle
1/4 teaspoon kosher salt
1/4 teaspoon lemon juice

FOR THE DUXELLES

2 tablespoons (1/4 stick) butter
2 cloves garlic, peeled and cut into
    paper-thin slices
1 shallot, peeled and brunoised
1/2 cup maitake mushrooms
1 (8-ounce) can cuitlacoche,
    cleaned
1/4 teaspoon salt
1/8 teaspoon chimayo chile

ANCHIOTE LAMB LOIN "WELLINGTON"

with Jalapeño Spoon Bread, Cuitlacoche Duxelles, Ancho Tomato Jus, and Tomato Mint Relish

In a deconstructed preparation inspired by the classic Beef Wellington, tender lamb is served atop a round of corn spoon bread with sautéed wild mushrooms on the side and a crown of baked pastry.

FOR THE SPOON BREAD

1 sweet corn ear
1 cup finely ground blue cornmeal
    (yellow cornmeal can be sub-
    stituted)
2 jalapeños, seeded and
    brunoised
4 eggs
1 tablespoon butter
2 cups heavy cream
2 cups whole milk

FOR THE LAMB

2 tablespoons annatto seed
2 teaspoons coriander
1 pound lamb loin
1 teaspoon salt

FOR THE CRUST

3 sheets feuille de brick

OPTIONAL GARNISH

Pasilla chile oil

To prepare the broth: combine all the ingredients in a saucepan and simmer over medium heat for 30 minutes. Season with salt, if needed, and strain through a fine chinois, letting the mixture drain naturally without pushing solids through; set aside.

To prepare the relish: combine all the ingredients in a small bowl and chill.

To prepare the duxelles: heat a sauté pan over low heat and add butter, garlic, and shallot; cook until translucent. Add the mushrooms and sauté until cooked through, about 4–6 minutes. Add the cuitlacoche, salt, and chile, then pull the pan off the heat. Use a knife to cut through the mixture until it resembles a coarse paste; set aside and keep warm.

To prepare the spoon bread: preheat the oven to 350 degrees F. Roast the ear of corn in the husk about 35 minutes. Cool and remove husk and all fibers. Slice corn off the cob. Lower the temperature of the oven to 325 degrees F. Combine all of the ingredients in the top of a double boiler and cook for approximately 15 minutes, stirring constantly until the mixture becomes thick. Place in a 5 x 9-inch baking dish lined with parchment and then coated with nonstick cooking spray. Bake, covered with foil, for 25 minutes, rotating every few minutes.

To prepare the lamb: grind the annatto and coriander in a spice grinder to a fine powder. Coat both sides of the lamb loin with this mixture and season with salt. Sear on medium-high heat to set the crust; do not allow the crust to burn.

To prepare the crust: preheat oven to 350 degrees F. Take three sheets of feuille de brick dough and lightly spray with nonstick cooking spray. Stack sheets and roll them together tightly. Cut the roll into 1/4-inch strips and divide into small "nests" on a baking sheet; bake for 12 minutes.

To serve the entrée: preheat the oven to 400 degrees F. Arrange the lamb loin on an ovenproof platter and cook for 3 minutes; top the loins with the duxelles, return to the oven, and cook for 1 minute more to heat the mushrooms. On a plate, place the lamb on top of the spoon bread and ladle some of the broth around it; garnish with the relish and top each piece of lamb with a pastry nest. Decorate the plate with pasilla chile oil if desired.

Wine Pairing E. Guigal Côte Rôtie Château d'Ampuis Syrah, Northern Rhône, France; or Ridge Geyserville Zinfandel, Sonoma County, California

Tasting Notes The earthy, savory elements of this dish pair well with a wine that has rich intensity.

MAKES 6 SERVINGS

FOR THE SORBET

1/2 cup packed Thai basil leaves
1 cup fresh lime juice
1 cup sugar
1 cup water

FOR THE TUILE

9 tablespoons butter
1-1/3 cups powdered sugar
4 egg whites
1-1/3 cups flour
Pinch of salt
1 tablespoon black sesame seeds

FOR THE GARNISH

1/4 cup raspberries
1/4 cup blackberries
1/4 cup premium sake*

*The Wild Sage kitchen uses Rihaku Dreamy Clouds Tokubetsu Junmai Nigori Sake, a fruity sweet sake from Matsue-shi, Shimane Prefecture, Japan.

BASIL LIME SORBET
with Black Sesame Tuile
and Dreamy Cloud Berries

A refreshing lime sorbet gets a hint of spiciness from fresh basil in this light dessert, accompanied by springtime berries and a crispy tuile cookie studded with black sesame seeds.

To prepare the sorbet, combine all the ingredients in a small saucepan and cook over medium-high heat until the mixture simmers. Strain the mixture and chill in the refrigerator for 4 hours. Process in an ice cream machine according to the manufacturer's directions. Freeze.

To prepare the tuile: preheat the oven to 350 degrees F and line a baking sheet with parchment paper. Using an electric mixer with the paddle attachment, cream the butter with the sugar in a medium bowl. Add the egg whites and scrape down the sides of the bowl; mix for 1 minute. With the mixer running, slowly add the flour and salt until a soft dough forms. Remove from the mixer and fold in sesame seeds by hand. Chill dough 10 minutes in the refrigerator. Fill a disposable pastry bag with the batter and pipe the mixture in cigar shapes onto the prepared baking sheet. Cook for 8 minutes, turning pan once so that the tuiles cook evenly. Use a thin spatula to remove the tuiles from the baking sheet and cool on a wire rack.

To serve the dessert: toss the berries gently in the sake. Place 2 scoops of the sorbet in a small martini glass and top with a spoonful of the berries. Garnish with the tuile.

MAKES 6 SERVINGS

FOR THE BLANCMANGE

4 gelatin sheets
1 cup peeled hazelnuts
2 cups heavy cream
1/4 cup hazelnut liqueur (such as
    Frangelico)
Seeds from 1 split, scraped
    vanilla bean
1/2 cup sugar

FOR THE SYRUP

1 cup huckleberries
1 cup water
1 cup sugar
Seeds from 1 split, scraped
    vanilla bean
1/2 cup ruby port wine

FOR THE COOKIES

9 tablespoons butter, softened
3/4 cup turbinado sugar
4 egg whites
1 pinch salt
2/3 cup flour

FOR THE GARNISH

Vanilla grass
Mint sprigs

HAZELNUT BLANCMANGE
with Huckleberry-Port Syrup
and Turbinado Sugar Cookie

Blancmange is a chilled, creamy French pudding that is the perfect backdrop for a sweet syrup made from just-picked Wyoming huckleberries.

To prepare the blancmange: bloom the gelatin sheets in cold water for 10 minutes. In a food processor fitted with a metal blade, process the hazelnuts, cream, and Frangelico for 1 minute. Strain the mixture through a fine mesh sieve and add to a tall-sided saucepan. Add the vanilla bean seeds and sugar to the mixture and bring to a simmer, stirring occasionally with a wooden spoon. Remove gelatin sheets and wring out excess water, add to cream mixture and stir to combine. Pour mixture into 6 lightly greased molds or custard cups and refrigerate overnight.

To prepare the syrup: combine all ingredients in a tall-sided saucepan and simmer over medium heat until small syrupy bubbles form and mixture is reduced by half. Transfer mixture to a blender and purée; strain through a fine mesh sieve and cool in the refrigerator.

To prepare the cookies: preheat oven to 350 degrees F. In a medium bowl, cream the butter with the sugar. Add the egg whites and salt, and then mix for 1 minute; scrape down the sides. With the mixer running, slowly add the flour until a dough forms. Chill the dough for 10 minutes in the refrigerator. Prepare a disposable pastry bag by trimming the pointed end to the approximate diameter of a pencil. Fill the pastry bag with the batter and pipe 7-inch lengths onto a parchment-lined baking sheet. Bake for 8 minutes, rotating once halfway through the cooking time, until cookies are light golden brown on the edges. Let cool on the pan to crisp.

To serve the dessert: place a stripe of the syrup in the center of each plate. Unmold the blancmange and place on top of the stripe. Garnish with a cookie, vanilla grass, and mint.

Huckleberry Heaven

Native Americans harvested huckleberries—which resemble blueberries—dried them, and used them for winter food and trade. Although many varieties of huckleberries exist, ranging in color from black to purple to red, the black huckleberry is common around Jackson Hole. Found at elevations from 2,000 to 11,500 feet, huckleberries can be ready for picking in late July or early August (depending on growing conditions) and are found on bushes along dirt roads and mountain trails. But don't expect a local to tell you the best place to find huckleberries; these locations are a closely guarded secret, often passed down from generation to generation. Huckleberries are an indigenous ingredient in Jackson Hole sauces, syrups, and jams. A local's favorite way of eating the tart berries is to drop them directly on ice cream or stir them into pancake batter.

Photo credit: Stock Photo

MAKES 6 SERVINGS

FOR THE ICE CREAM

1/2 cup sugar

6 egg yolks

2 cups heavy cream

Seeds from 1 split, scraped
vanilla bean

1 ounce (2 tablespoons) ground
espresso, tied in a cheesecloth
"sachet"

FOR THE BEIGNETS

1/2 cup sugar

1 egg

1/2 cup buttermilk

2 tablespoons butter, melted

2 cups sifted flour

2 teaspoons baking powder

1 quart canola oil for frying

FOR THE CINNAMON SUGAR

1/4 teaspoon cinnamon

2 tablespoons sugar

FOR THE HOT CHOCOLATE

3/4 cup cream

1/4 pound dark chocolate

2 ounces Mexican Barra chocolate

FOR THE GARNISH

18 chocolate-covered espresso
beans

CINNAMON BEIGNETS
with Espresso Ice Cream and Hot Chocolate

Warm, crispy cinnamon-sugar-coated beignets are served with a frosty, house-made coffee ice cream in this updated take on a Southern favorite. Mexican Barra chocolate flavors the warm sauce that is drizzled on top.

To prepare the ice cream: set up a double boiler with a metal mixing bowl. Mix the sugar and egg yolks with a whisk until pale yellow and fluffy. Add the cream, vanilla bean seeds, and espresso sachet, and cook on a double boiler to 175 degrees F. Strain and chill the mixture in the refrigerator for 4 hours, then process in an ice cream machine according to the manufacturer's directions.

To prepare the beignets: beat the sugar and egg until light, fluffy, and pale yellow. Add the buttermilk and butter to the mixture. Combine the flour and baking powder in a small bowl and add to the mixture; stir just until combined but do not overmix. Let rest for 20 minutes in the refrigerator. On a flat floured surface, roll out the dough to 1/4 thickness and cut out 1-1/2-inch rounds. Cover and set aside until ready to finish.

To prepare the cinnamon sugar: mix both ingredients together; set aside.

To prepare the hot chocolate: scald the cream in a saucepan. Chop the chocolates and add to the scalded cream. Remove from the heat and let rest for 3 minutes. Using a whisk, mix until all ingredients are homogenous and smooth; set aside and keep warm.

To finish the beignets: heat the canola oil in a tall-sided pot fitted with a candy thermometer to 375 degrees F. Working in batches, fry the beignets for about 1 minute per side, until golden brown. Remove and drain on a tray lined with paper towels. Toss the beignets in the cinnamon sugar.

To serve the dessert: Arrange beignets on each plate with a scoop of the ice cream. Drizzle with the warm chocolate and garnish with espresso beans.

AUTUMN ARRIVES

Yellowstone National Park

Climb the mountains

and get their good tidings.

Nature's peace will flow into you

as sunshine flows into trees.

The winds will blow

their own freshness into you,

and the storms their energy,

while cares drop off like autumn leaves.

John Muir, Naturalist

Yellowstone, 1885

IN THE VALLEY, the shift from summer to fall is subtle. One morning in late August, the light becomes softer, more golden, and the air holds a chill that wasn't there the day before. Residents watch for that first gold leaf to appear, and soon the hills are splashed with red, gold, and orange. The eerie calls of bugling elk echo off the mountain walls—a traditional autumn evening song in Jackson Hole.

For many in Jackson, fall is a favorite season, as the summer crowds scatter with the falling leaves. But don't imagine autumn as a sedentary time—quite the contrary. Weather prevailing, locals take to the hills—getting in those last hikes, bike rides, and floats on the river before winter's first flakes appear. Some of the best fishing on the Snake River arrives in fall, and kayaking the Moran Oxbow amidst the golden trees lining the banks provides a memorable highlight of the season. Bikers take back the roads, exploring without the impediment of summer's busy automobile traffic. Fall also offers a popular time for viewing wildlife

in the area as bull elk bugle to attract their harems and bears forage in preparation for their long winter naps.

Many years ago, Jackson cleared out in September—with the historic wooden sidewalks empty, parking spaces around the Town Square plentiful, and hotels with rooms to spare. But the sparkling transitional season is quiet no longer, thanks to the Jackson Hole Fall Arts Festival. Established in 1985, the festival provides a much-anticipated social and cultural event with two weeks of arts-centered activities, including gallery strolls, art auctions, live performances on the Town Square, and that roundup of Jackson Hole's culinary arts—Taste of the Tetons. Adding to the event's artistic cachet, the Western Design Conference joins the Fall Arts Festival lineup. The world's preeminent juried exhibition of western furniture, home accessories, and fashion showcases the innovative methods and materials of top artisans working in wood, metal, textiles, and more—interpreting the West through designs ranging from rustic to contemporary.

Fall in Jackson Hole provides a feast for the senses: the scent of wood smoke, the sound of leaves crunching underfoot, the sight of the mountains' colorful palette, and the taste of homemade huckleberry preserves, ready for the pantry. The chill air inspires heartier restaurant fare as preserves, root vegetables, and game are prepared for the winter larder.

At the Wild Sage, the lengthening shadows of bright Indian summer days and autumn's cooler nights inspire a new menu that celebrates the flavors, textures, and colors of the changing seasons. Warm soups might feature golden corn from the final harvest, enlivened with roasted green chiles, or bright orange sweet potatoes in a smooth bisque, paired with zingy red curry and fresh blue crab. Salads are heartier; menus might include bitter greens tossed with ingredients like shaved cheese, sun-dried cranberries, or crunchy toasted almonds—or perhaps a perfect plate of lightly dressed crisp-tender haricots verts.

Meats like duck, game, and ribs are welcome additions to the restaurant's offerings, and seafood like mussels flown in fresh from Prince Edward Island might appear on the menu in a Spanish-inspired saffron-based broth. Comforting homespun desserts are prepared with the Wild Sage's trademark flair: fresh ginger infuses a moist carrot cake served with cream cheese gelato, and crisp autumn apples are slow-cooked for chutney that tops a "bread" pudding made with flaky croissants.

National Museum of Wildlife Art: A Walk on the Wild Side

Wildlife viewing in Jackson Hole comes year-round and in many locales—including indoors. The National Museum of Wildlife Art (www.wildlifeart.org) is unique among American art museums, with its collection of more than 5,000 catalog items focused exclusively on wildlife and humanity's relationship with nature, with changing exhibitions and programs. Situated on a butte just outside Jackson, the museum overlooks the 25,000-acre National Elk Refuge and is en route to Grand Teton and Yellowstone National Parks. Fittingly, the museum preserves and interprets this art in one of the few remaining areas of the U.S. where native wildlife still roams abundantly and free.

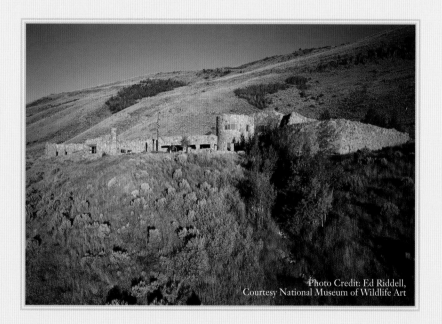

Photo Credit: Ed Riddell,
Courtesy National Museum of Wildlife Art

Elk and Wolves and Bears—Oh, My!

Elk-bugling reaches its peak during autumn months as massive bull elk round up and guard their harems, their eerie cries ringing through the dusk. Meanwhile, bears and wolves are hunting in Yellowstone's wildlife-rich Lamar and Hayden Valleys in preparation for the coming winter, attracted by the large concentrations of elk. The area offers ideal viewing opportunities for all three large mammals—a chance to see both predators and prey in their natural habitat—in addition to the magnificent autumn colors of Yellowstone. Rusty Parrot Lodge guests who prefer a self-guided tour are just a short drive from the park (but will want to spend a night or two in the park to take in all the sights). Those who prefer to leave the driving to someone else can take advantage of the expert guides at Wildlife Expeditions, a renowned wildlife tour company that provides two- and three-day wildlife tours of Yellowstone.

Art in the Hole: Jackson Hole Fall Arts Festival

Recognized as one of the premiere art events in the Rocky Mountain West, the Jackson Hole Fall Arts Festival hosts world-class installments of visual, contemporary, culinary, western, landscape, wildlife, and Native American arts for three weeks each September. The popular festival boasts more than fifty events, including gallery walks, workshops, and artist receptions. Particular crowd-pleasers include "Taste of the Tetons," allowing participants to stroll and sample food, wine, and dessert from top Jackson Hole chefs in the heart of historic downtown Jackson; the annual QuickDraw Art Sale and Auction, where inspiration flows fast and furious as artists create original works while spectators watch; and the festival's latest addition, the Western Design Conference, the preeminent exhibition of western furniture, fashion, and accessories by top artisans.

MAKES 6 SERVINGS

FOR THE BISQUE

1 tablespoon red curry paste
1/2 tablespoon canola oil
3 cups peeled and diced fresh yams
    or sweet potatoes
4 cloves garlic, peeled and minced
2 shallots, peeled and chopped
1 ginger lobe, peeled and minced
1 lemongrass stalk, bruised
    and cut into 3-inch lengths
14 ounces coconut milk
    (not coconut cream)
4 cups chicken stock (see Source
    Directory page 213 for recipe)
1/4 teaspoon salt
1 teaspoon Thai fish sauce

FOR THE CRÈME FRAÎCHE

1 teaspoon wasabi powder
1/2 cup heavy cream
1 teaspoon buttermilk

FOR THE GARNISH

1/2 pound lump crabmeat, picked
    through to remove any shell
    fragments
Basil leaf chiffonade (about
    6 leaves)

ROASTED CAMOTE BISQUE
with Coconut and Red Curry Broth and Wasabi Crème Fraîche

This smooth Thai-influenced bisque is made from yams, also known as camote in some Latin cultures. A swirl of wasabi-spiked crème fraîche provides a zingy kick to the soup, which is finished with tender crabmeat and a fragrant garnish of fresh basil.

To prepare the bisque: toast the curry paste over medium heat with the oil. Add the yams, garlic, shallots, ginger, lemongrass, coconut milk, and stock. Let simmer for 25 minutes until the yams are cooked and quite tender. Add the salt and Thai fish sauce, and correct seasonings if necessary. Purée in a blender and reserve warm.

To prepare the crème fraîche: combine all the ingredients in a nonreactive bowl. Let the bowl stay out at room temperature overnight, covered loosely.

To serve the soup: preheat the oven to 350 degrees F. Heat the crabmeat for 4 minutes in a small baking pan. Spoon equal portions of the crab in the center of each bowl, top with the basil and ladle the bisque around it. Garnish with the wasabi cream and serve immediately.

MAKES 6–8 SERVINGS

FOR THE CHOWDER

3 bacon strips, cut into small pieces

2 celery ribs, diced (1/2-inch cubes)

1 onion, diced (1/2-inch cubes)

1 carrot, diced (1/2-inch cubes)

3 Anaheim chiles, roasted, skinned, and seeded

3 cloves garlic

2 tablespoons butter

1 potato

4 sweet corn ears, roasted and kernels removed

2 tablespoons flour

4 cups chicken stock

2 cups cream

FOR THE RELISH

1 cup chayote pepper

1 tablespoon oil

1/8 teaspoon salt

1/8 teaspoon pepper

1 tablespoon cilantro chiffonade

2 tablespoons red bell pepper brunoise

CHARRED CORN AND GREEN CHILE CHOWDER
with Grilled Chayote Relish

Perfect for enjoying the season's late corn harvest, this creamy soup gets a kick from roasted Anaheim chiles as well as a garnish of chayote peppers enlivened with fresh cilantro.

To prepare the chowder: render the bacon in a large saucepan over low heat. Remove the bacon from the pan with a slotted spoon and drain on paper towels. Add the celery, onion, carrot, chiles, garlic, and butter to the pan, and cook until vegetables are translucent. Add the potato, corn, and flour, and then stir and cook 6 minutes; deglaze pan with the stock. Add cream and slowly bring to a simmer.

To prepare the relish: slice the chayote into 1/4-inch slices and toss in oil, salt, and pepper; grill over high heat for 2 minutes per side, turning twice. Let cool and cut into 1/4-inch dice. Toss with cilantro and bell pepper; set aside and keep warm.

To serve the soup: ladle chowder into bowls and garnish with relish.

FOR THE DRESSING

3 cloves garlic, peeled

2 anchovies

1/4 teaspoon sriracha

2 tablespoons lemon juice

2 tablespoons Dijon mustard

1 tablespoon finely grated Grana Padano cheese

1 egg

1/4 teaspoon black pepper

2/3 cup extra virgin olive oil

FOR THE "FRICO"

2 cups finely grated Grana Padano cheese

FOR THE SALAD

1 small head sweet Valentine lettuce, washed, dried, and gently torn into pieces

1 small head green forest lettuce, washed, dried, and gently torn into pieces (or substitute petite heads of Romaine lettuce)

SWEET VALENTINE AND GREEN FOREST LETTUCE
with Creamy Garlic Dressing and Grana Padano "Frico"

A sophisticated take on Caesar salad combines tender baby lettuces with a creamy anchovy-laced dressing; instead of croutons, the salad is topped with a savory "chip" made of baked cheese.

To prepare the dressing: combine all the ingredients except the oil in a blender. Process for 1 minute. Slowly emulsify oil into the mixture.

To prepare the "frico": preheat oven to 325 degrees F. Line an ovenproof pan with parchment paper. Portion the cheese into 2-inch rounds, as thin as possible. Bake for 12 minutes, turning once. Remove from pan and let cool.

To serve the salad: dress the lettuce, divide evenly between 6 plates, and garnish with the "frico."

FOR THE VINAIGRETTE

1/2 cup fresh orange
    juice (reserve zest from
    oranges used below)
1 vanilla bean, scraped
1 shallot, peeled and chopped
2 cloves garlic, peeled and chopped
1/4 cup champagne vinegar
2 tablespoons sugar
1/2 teaspoon salt
1 cup olive oil
1 cup canola oil

FOR THE CRISP

1/2 pound Vella Jack cheese, finely
    grated by hand (reserve about
    4 tablespoons for the garnish)

FOR THE ZEST

1/2 cup sugar
1/2 cup water
3 oranges, skin zested, fruit
    supremed for the garnish

**FOR THE SALAD
AND GARNISH**

1/2 pound (about 1 cup)
    Marcona almonds
1 pound fresh rocket greens
    (arugula), washed and dried
3 orange supremes
2 ounces (about 4 tablespoons)
    sun-dried cranberries

ROCKET SALAD
with Orange Vanilla Vinaigrette, Orange Supremes, Vella Jack Crisp, Marcona Almonds, and Sun-Dried Cranberries

This salad is full of texture and flavor, with bitter greens complemented by a sweet orange-based dressing, crunchy roasted almonds, sweet-sour dried cranberries, and a savory cheese crisp.

To prepare the vinaigrette: place all the ingredients in a blender except the olive and canola oils. While processing on high, slowly pour the oils into the mixture until fully emulsified.

To prepare the crisp: preheat oven to 325 degrees F. Line an ovenproof pan with parchment paper. Portion the cheese into 1 x 3-inch rectangles, as thin as possible. Bake for 12 minutes, turning once. Remove from pan and let cool.

To prepare the zest: combine the sugar and water in a saucepan and bring to a simmer. Add the zest to the liquid, simmer for 4 minutes, then remove from heat and let rest in the liquid for 1 hour. Strain and place on a sheet pan in a single layer to dry and crisp.

To serve the salad: preheat oven to 350 degrees F. Roast the almonds, turning every 2 minutes for 12 minutes total; let cool and become crisp. Lightly dress the greens with the vinaigrette, divide into individual portions, and place each portion in the center of a plate. Arrange the supremed tangerines around the greens. Sprinkle the salad with almonds, cranberries, and grated cheese. Top each salad with a crisp.

MAKES 4 SERVINGS

FOR THE PORK

2 pounds pork belly, cleaned

2 tablespoons brown sugar

1 teaspoon salt

2 tablespoons green curry

1 parsnip, diced (1/2-inch cubes)

1 carrot, diced (1/2-inch cubes)

2 ginger lobes, chopped

1-1/2 cups sake

FOR THE SUCCOTASH

2 corn ears (about 1 cup kernels)

1 tablespoon + 1 teaspoon butter

1 serrano chile, sliced

1 teaspoon minced garlic

2 shallots, peeled and diced
   (1/2-inch cubes)

1 cup cooked and shelled edamame

1/2 teaspoon salt

2 tablespoons red pepper

1/8 teaspoon white pepper

1/4 cup chicken stock

SAKE AND GREEN CURRY–BRAISED PORK BELLY

with Edamame Succotash, Fried Quail Eggs, and Apricot-Shallot Glaze

Bacon lovers will find plenty to appreciate with this unusual pairing of slow-roasted pork belly accompanied by a spicy edamame-corn succotash.

FOR THE SAUCE

1 cup red wine vinegar

2 cloves garlic, peeled and minced

2 shallots, peeled and minced

1 ginger lobe, peeled
   and minced (enough
   to make 1/4 cup)

18 ounces (about 2-1/4 cups)
   apricot preserves

1/4 cup packed chopped cilantro

2 tablespoons soy sauce

FOR THE QUAIL EGGS

1 tablespoon butter

1 tablespoon extra virgin
   olive oil

1 dozen quail eggs

FOR THE GARNISH

1 tablespoon sweet
   soy sauce

Microgreens or baby basil

To prepare the pork: rub the belly with the sugar, salt, and green curry, and place in an ovenproof pan. Arrange the parsnip, carrot, and ginger around the belly; pour the sake over the pork and vegetables. Let marinate in the refrigerator overnight. Preheat oven to 290 degrees F, cover the pan with aluminum foil, and roast the pork belly for 4 hours. Remove the foil and cook for 1 more hour. Let cool in the refrigerator overnight. The next day, trim the pork belly into 2 x 2-inch squares, reserving all scraps for the succotash.

To prepare the succotash: preheat the oven to 350 degrees F; roast the corn in the oven 40 minutes in husk. Remove corn kernels from the cobs. Chop the pork belly scraps into 1/4-inch dice. Heat a sauté pan over medium-high heat and add the pork belly. Cook until some of the fat is rendered, then add 1 tablespoon of the butter and the serrano, garlic, and shallots; cook until translucent. Deglaze the pan with the stock and add the edamame. Cook for 3 minutes and add the corn, salt, and red and white peppers. Add the chicken stock, cook for 3 minutes, and remove from heat. Cool briefly and add the remaining 1 teaspoon butter, stirring just until melted.

To prepare the sauce: heat a small saucepan over medium heat. Add vinegar, garlic, shallots, and ginger, and reduce by three-fourths. While the reduction is cooking, purée the apricot preserves in a blender. Add the purée to the saucepan and bring to a simmer. Add the cilantro and soy sauce, take the pan off the heat, and steep mixture for 5 minutes. Push the mixture through a sieve and reserve warm.

To prepare the quail eggs: In a medium-size sauté pan, melt the butter and olive oil over medium heat. (Be careful not to overheat the pan because the eggs will burn easily.) Quail egg shells are harder than chicken egg shells, so crack them open by giving them a quick, sharp tap with the blade of a small knife and separating the halves. Fry the quail eggs 4 at a time and remove to a heated plate tented with aluminum foil; reserve.

To serve the appetizer: preheat the oven to 375 degrees F. Heat the pork in the oven on an ovenproof pan for 8 minutes. Pull from the oven, coat the pork with the sauce, and return to the oven for an additional 4 minutes. To serve, spoon some of the succotash on each of 4 plates and top each plate with 3 pieces of the pork belly. Arrange a fried quail egg on each piece of pork belly and top with microgreens. Garnish the plates with the sweet soy sauce.

Wine Pairing Eric Forest Macon-Vergisson "Sur la Roche," Burgundy, France

Tasting Notes This wine pairs well with the heat from the green curry, the sweetness of the apricots and shallots, and the succulence of the succotash.

MAKES 4–6 SERVINGS

FOR THE CROQUETTES

2 cups fava beans
6 cups water
1 cup stemmed parsley
1/8 cup lemon juice
1 tablespoon coriander
1/2 teaspoon salt
3 cloves garlic
Canola oil

FOR THE CAVIAR

1 medium eggplant
1/2 teaspoon sugar
1/2 teaspoon salt
1 tablespoon lemon juice
6 tablespoons tahini
4 tablespoons olive oil

FOR THE TABBOULEH

1/2 cup quinoa
1 cup water
3 Roma tomatoes, diced (1/4-inch
    cubes)
1/2 cup chopped onion
Mint leaf chiffonade (about
    20 mint leaves)
1 cup chopped parsley
1/2 teaspoon salt
1 tablespoon olive oil
1 tablespoon lemon juice

ALEPPO-DUSTED LAMB
with Quinoa and Mint Tabbouleh, Eggplant Caviar, and Fava Bean Croquette

Lamb loin gets a spicy kick from a coating of ground aleppo peppers, which lend a fruitiness and mild cumin-like flavor to the dish. Fava beans, the legumes made famous in the movie *Silence of the Lambs*, are shaped into tender cakes, fried to a crispy brown, and accompanied by a Middle Eastern–influenced quinoa-based tabbouleh.

FOR THE LAMB

1 pound boneless lamb loin, cut
    into 3-ounce portions
2 tablespoons aleppo
1 tablespoon coriander
1/2 teaspoon salt
2 tablespoons olive oil

FOR THE GARNISH

6 mint sprigs
4 tablespoons pomegranate
    molasses

To prepare the croquettes: soak the fava beans in the water overnight in the refrigerator. Peel the thick husks and discard; discard any beans that can't be peeled. In a food processor, add all ingredients and pulse into a coarse paste, but do not purée. The soaking liquid can be used to loosen the mixture if needed. Portion into 2-ounce rounds and set aside.

To prepare the caviar: preheat the oven to 350 degrees F and cook the eggplant for 1 hour. Remove it from he oven, cool briefly, and then wrap the entire eggplant in plastic wrap. Allow to cool to room temperature. Cut the choke end off the eggplant, roughly chop the remaining eggplant, and transfer it to a strainer. Sprinkle with sugar and salt, and let drain for 20 minutes. Discard the juice and process the eggplant with all other ingredients except the oil in a food processor. With the motor running, slowly drizzle the oil into the mixture until it is fully emulsified. Set aside at room temperature.

To prepare the tabbouleh: rinse the quinoa and combine it with the water in a saucepan. Cook over medium-high heat until it simmers, reduce the heat, and simmer it for 15 minutes, or until tender. Cool to room temperature; then combine it with the tomatoes, onion, mint, parsley, and salt in a mixing bowl. Add the olive oil and lemon juice just before serving.

To prepare the lamb: preheat a heavy-bottomed sauté pan over medium heat. Coat all sides of the lamb with the seasonings. Sear both sides in the oil, making sure not to burn the crust. Finish in the oven at 400 degrees F for 2 minutes. Remove from oven and let rest for 5 minutes.

To finish the croquettes: pour two inches of canola oil in a tall-sided saucepan and heat to 375 degrees F; fry the croquettes for 4 minutes, until dark golden brown and floating. Set aside on a platter lined with paper towels.

To serve the appetizer: place the tabbouleh in the center of each plate and top with a croquette. Spoon some eggplant caviar on the croquette and place the sliced lamb on top. Garnish with mint sprigs and pomegranate molasses.

Wine Pairing Barrua, Isola dei Nuragi, Sardinia, Italy

Tasting Notes This wine complements the strong Middle Eastern influences and fresh flavors of the tabbouleh.

MAKES 4–6 SERVINGS

2 pounds Pei Black mussels,
    debearded and cleaned

1/4 pound linguiça sausage, sliced
    and browned

1 cup clam juice

1/2 teaspoon crushed saffron
    strands (crushed with fingers)

1 large shallot, peeled and
    brunoised (about 2 tablespoons)

5 cloves Spanish Roja garlic (or sub-
    stitute regular garlic), peeled
    and minced

3 Roma tomatoes, diced (1/4-inch
    cubes), divided

1 tablespoon fresh oregano,
    leaves only

PRINCE EDWARD ISLAND MUSSELS
with Saffron, Roja Garlic, and Linguiça Sausage

A perennially popular appetizer at the Wild Sage, fresh black mussels are quickly steamed and served with a garlicky Mediterranean-style broth perfect for soaking up with crusty bread.

To prepare the mussels: put the mussels, sausage, clam juice, saffron, shallot, garlic, and two-thirds of the tomatoes into a large saucepan. Cover and cook over very high heat for 3 minutes. Remove the lid and stir the mussels; continue cooking for 2 more minutes, or until all the mussels are open. Toss in half of the oregano and remove from the heat.

To serve: spoon some of the garlic mixture into each bowl; top with some of the mussels, the remaining tomato, and the oregano.

Wine Pairing suggestion: Domaine de Chantemerle Chablis Premier Cru Fourchaumes, Burgundy, France

Tasting Notes This is a very classical pairing.

Microgreens: Diminutive Size, Big Flavor

The Wild Sage kitchen frequently requests microgreens from its purveyors; the miniature greens are actually baby seedlings from vegetables and greens with a concentrated flavor and bright green color that are used for garnishes or added to salads. Microgreens may not be readily available at retail stores, but home cooks can grow their own from seed; turnip, cabbage, kale, arugula, radish, and kohlrabi are all popular varieties that can be easily started in a moist growing medium in a sunny location. The microgreens are generally harvested just after they form their first true leaves.

Sandy Harrison's Chocolate Mole Sauce

Growing up in Texas, I came to Jackson Hole with a wonderful collection of Tex-Mex recipes that were passed down through my family. I wanted to include this one to honor the many Hispanic employees we have, whose friendship and dedication we cherish. Mexico's rich and diverse culinary traditions include countless complex and vibrant dishes. This simple Chocolate Mole (a word meaning "sauce" or "mixture") can be used in enchiladas or as a sauce over pork, chicken, or cheese dishes. This is one of our family's favorites, and I promise that you will feel like it's a fiesta when you use it on a Mexican dish.

From our family to yours,

Sandy Harrison

MAKES APPROXIMATELY 5 CUPS

7 saltine crackers

1 tablespoon vegetable oil

3 dried bay leaves

1 cinnamon stick

4 cups water

1 teaspoon salt

7 dried mild Pasilla peppers, stems and seeds removed

6 mild Japone peppers, stems and seeds removed

3 cubes authentic Mexican chocolate (I use Nestle Abuelita brand)

To prepare the mole: in a blender or food processor, process the saltines, vegetable oil, bay leaves, cinnamon stick, water, and salt. Scrape down the sides of the blender and add the chile peppers; process until the mixture is puréed.

Put the chocolate in a large, heavy frying pan over medium heat. Press the chile mixture with a wooden spoon through a medium mesh sieve into the frying pan. Cook, stirring constantly, until chocolate is melted and the mixture is heated through.

MAKES 6 SERVINGS

FOR THE DUCK

6 fresh rosemary sprigs
1 tablespoon loose green tea
6 duck breasts
1/2 teaspoon salt
1/2 teaspoon freshly ground black
    pepper

FOR THE CABBAGE

4 tablespoons butter
3 cinnamon sticks
1 head purple cabbage, sliced
1/4 cup raspberry vinegar
1 cup water
1/4 cup sugar

FOR THE JUS

2 cups pomegranate jus
1/2 cup veal stock

FOR THE GARNISH

Canola oil for frying
1 sweet potato, peeled and thinly
    julienned on a mandoline

FOR THE GNOCCHI

1 large sweet potato
1 cup grated Sage Derby Cheese
1 egg
3/4 cup flour
1 teaspoon salt, divided
1 quart water
2 tablespoons butter

ROSEMARY- AND GREEN TEA–SMOKED DUCK BREAST
with Sweet Potato–Sage Gnocchi and Pomegranate Jus

This recipe utilizes a quick smoking method perfect for
home cooks who don't own a stovetop or stand-alone smoker.
Duck is smoked in an aromatic mixture of fresh rosemary
and green tea, and is accompanied by tender gnocchi made
with sweet potatoes and sweet-sour raspberry-braised cabbage.

To prepare the duck: use a heavy-bottomed ovenproof pan with a fitted resting rack and put it on the stovetop over low heat. Add the rosemary and green tea directly to the bottom of the pan and then fit the resting rack with the duck breast on top; sprinkle with salt and pepper. Cover the pan with foil and make two pinholes. Heat on low until smoke comes through the holes. Make sure to move the pan evenly on the burner. Smoke for 5 minutes, then pull off the heat and let sit covered for 5 minutes. Remove duck and discard rosemary and green tea. In a separate cold sauté pan, place the duck breast fat-side-down and render on medium heat.

To prepare the cabbage: melt the butter in a large saucepan with the cinnamon sticks. Add cabbage and cook over medium heat for 5 minutes. Deglaze with vinegar and add water and sugar. Cook on low heat for 25–30 minutes, or until liquid is reduced by 90 percent. Remove cinnamon sticks and set aside.

To prepare jus: combine both ingredients in a saucepan and simmer over medium heat for 30 minutes, or until the mixture is reduced to about 1 cup; set aside and keep warm.

To prepare the garnish: heat the oil to 320 degrees F and fry the sweet potato shoestrings until the oil stops bubbling; drain on a tray lined with paper towels in a single layer; let air-dry and crisp for at least 1 hour.

To prepare the gnocchi: bake the sweet potato at 350 degrees F for 1 to 1-1/2 hours, or until tender and cooked thoroughly. Peel and mash the sweet potato; in a medium bowl, mix it with the cheese, egg, flour, and 1/2 teaspoon of salt to make a dough. Wrap the dough in plastic wrap and chill it for 20 minutes.

Heat a tall-sided saucepan with the water and the remaining 1/2 teaspoon of salt, and bring to a boil. Once the dough is chilled, roll it out on a floured work surface into 3/4-inch ropes. Cut each rope into 1-inch pieces, then press each piece of dough against the tines of a fork to create ridges.

Create an ice bath to shock the cooked gnocchi. Working in batches, cook the gnocchi in a pan of boiling water until they float, about 2 minutes. Shock the cooked gnocchi immediately in the ice bath. Remove from the ice bath after 3 minutes; allow to drain. Heat a sauté pan with the butter and sauté the gnocchi for 3–4 minutes until golden brown and crisp on at least one side.

To serve the entrée: use a large, low-sided bowl for each serving. Spoon some of the cabbage in the center of the bowl. Slice the warm duck into 4 pieces on the bias. Fan the duck around one side of the cabbage. Arrange the gnocchi on the opposite side of the dish and ladle the jus around the gnocchi and on the duck breast.

Wine Pairing **Perrot-Minot Vosne Romanée "Au Dessus de la Riviere," Burgundy, France**

Tasting Notes **Duck with Pinot Noir is a classical pairing, but we need something with some earthiness and a fair amount of complexity to balance the rich fattiness of the duck.**

MAKES 8 SERVINGS

FOR THE CRUST

2 star anise pods

2 tablespoons whole coriander

4 tablespoons whole black
   peppercorns

FOR THE ELK

2 pounds elk short loin, denuded

3 cloves garlic, halved

1 shallot, cut into
   1/2-inch slices

1 thumb-sized ginger lobe, peeled
   and chopped

1 bunch cilantro, roughly chopped

2 cups canola oil

FOR THE PURÉE

7 parsnips, diced (1/2-inch cubes)

2 quarts water

1/4 cup cream

1 tablespoon butter

1/2 teaspoon salt

1/8 teaspoon ground white pepper

FOR THE REDUCTION

5 cups apple cider

1 cup lingonberries

1 tablespoon Szechuan
   peppercorns

NORTH AMERICAN ELK AU POIVRE
with Parsnip Purée and Lingonberry Reduction

Hearty and rich, pan-seared elk steaks are served with

a creamy purée of parsnips and a slow-cooled lingonberry

sauce that gets a kick from Szechuan peppercorns.

To prepare the crust: grind anise first into a powder in a spice grinder. Then add coriander and pepper and grind into a coarse grind.

To prepare the elk: portion the loins into 8 (6-ounce) pieces. Mix remaining ingredients with the canola oil and pour over the elk portions; cover and refrigerate overnight, turning once.

To prepare the purée: remove the woody core of parsnips and discard. Heat the water to boiling in a large pan and cook the parsnips for 12–18 minutes, or until tender; let drain completely. Process parsnips in a food mill. Heat cream and butter in a saucepan over medium heat until butter is melted, then fold into parsnips. Season with salt and white pepper.

To prepare the reduction: combine all the ingredients in a medium saucepan and cook over medium-high heat until the mixture is reduced by 90 percent and small syrupy bubbles form.

To serve the entrée: preheat a large cast-iron skillet. Discard the marinade and coat the elk portions with the crust mixture. Sear the elk on high heat, 2 minutes per side. Finish the steaks in a preheated 400 degree F oven to desired temperature and let rest for 4 minutes. Slice the elk on the bias and place in the center of the plate; drizzle the reduction around the steak. Spoon some of the purée next to the elk.

Wine Pairing Domaine la Bouissiere Gigondas, Southern Rhone Valley, France

Tasting Notes The spicy red fruit nose of the wine pairs well with the elk's hearty flavor and cracked pepper coating.

MAKES 4–6 SERVINGS

FOR THE RIBS

4 pounds Snake River Farms baby
back ribs

3 quarts water

1-1/2 tablespoons salt

1 tablespoon granulated sugar

2 sprigs thyme

2 sprigs rosemary

1 shallot, peeled and quartered

8 cloves garlic, peeled

2 quarts oil

FOR THE GRITS

2 rosemary sprigs

2-1/2 cups water

1 cup chicken stock

1-1/4 cups coarse white polenta

1 tablespoon butter

3/4 cup heavy cream

1/2 cup grated white cheddar
cheese

1/2 teaspoon salt

1/8 teaspoon white pepper

FOR THE GLAZE

2 cups sun-dried cranberries

1/2 cup white balsamic vinegar

4 cups water

1/2 cup sugar

GARNISH

Steamed cauliflower florets

CONFIT OF BABY BACK RIBS
With Cranberry-Balsamic Glaze
and Rosemary White Cheddar Grits

While duck is the traditional meat used in the slow-cooked
confit preparation, here the Wild Sage chef uses baby back
ribs in the rich dish and accompanies it with creamy polenta.
A sweet-sour cranberry glaze provides the perfect balance
of flavors.

To prepare the ribs: cut them in half and rinse under cold water for 2 minutes. Combine all the ingredients except the oil and pour over the ribs in a large nonreactive dish. Cover and allow the ribs to marinate in the brine in the refrigerator for 24 hours, turning occasionally. Remove the ribs and rinse with cold water, then pat dry.

Preheat the oven to 290 degrees F. Arrange the ribs in an ovenproof dish and pour the oil over them. Seal the pan with aluminum foil and cook in the oven for 5 hours. Let the ribs cool in the oil overnight. Remove the ribs and discard the oil. Using a kitchen towel, gently rub off excess oil and the connective tissue from the back of the rack and portion into 2 bone racks; reserve on a warm platter tented with aluminum foil.

To prepare the grits: add the rosemary, water, and chicken stock to a medium saucepan and heat to boiling. Remove the rosemary and add the polenta; cook over low heat, stirring constantly, for about 5 minutes, or until almost all the liquid is absorbed. Add the butter and cream; heat for 1 minute, stirring constantly, and then remove from the heat. Stir in the cheese and season with salt and pepper.

To prepare the glaze: combine all the ingredients in a small saucepan and cook over medium-high heat until reduced by half. Remove from the heat, cool, and then process in a blender until smooth. Push the mixture through a fine mesh sieve; set aside and keep warm.

To serve the entrée: spoon some of the grits in a circle on the plate. Top each serving with 2 ribs and drizzle the glaze over the top. Garnish with the cauliflower.

Wine Pairing Borsao Tres Picos (Old Vine) Garnacha, Borja, Spain

Tasting Notes We need a big rich wine to pair with this meal, as there is such richness and intensity here plus the acidity of cranberry and balsamic, which would ruin many weaker wines.

MAKES 8 SERVINGS

FOR THE PUDDING

6 egg yolks
1/2 cup sugar
2 cups heavy cream
1 vanilla bean, split and scraped
Pinch of salt
3 regular-size croissants, baked and
    diced (1/2-inch cubes)

FOR THE CRÈME ANGLAISE

1 cup heavy cream
1 vanilla bean, split and scraped
Pinch of salt
3 egg yolks
1/4 cup sugar

FOR THE CHUTNEY

1 tablespoon butter
2 apples, peeled and diced
    (1/4-inch cubes)
1/2 cup apple brandy (such as
    Calvados)
1 cup water
1/3 cup brown sugar
2 cinnamon sticks
1/4 teaspoon lemon juice

FOR THE CARAMEL SHARDS

1 cup water
1 cup sugar

FOR THE GARNISH

1 cup whipped cream
8 mint sprigs

CROISSANT BREAD PUDDING
with Brandied Apple Chutney, Caramel Shards, and Crème Anglaise

Flaky croissants are used in this over-the-top version of "bread" pudding, accompanied by homemade apple chutney enlivened with Calvados brandy. The elements of the recipe can be prepared ahead of time and assembled at the last minute for a perfect ending to an autumn meal.

To prepare the pudding: preheat the oven to 300 degrees F. Combine egg yolks and sugar with a wire whisk until pale yellow. Add all other ingredients and mix well to combine. Soak the croissants in custard mixture for at least 1 hour. Lightly grease an 8 x 8-inch baking pan and fill with the pudding mixture. Prepare a water bath and cook for 1 hour 15 minutes; let cool.

To prepare the crème anglaise: scald the cream with the vanilla bean and salt. In a metal mixing bowl, cream together the yolks and sugar until light yellow. Add prepared cream to temper the yolks. Make a double boiler and cook mixture, constantly stirring, until it reaches 175 degrees F and will coat the back of a spoon; strain and chill.

To prepare the chutney: heat the butter over medium-high heat in a large sauté pan. Add the apples and cook for 6 minutes. Deglaze the pan with the brandy. Add all other ingredients and simmer for 20 minutes; reserve warm.

To prepare the caramel shards: combine the water and sugar in a small saucepan and heat on high. Once a deep amber color is achieved, remove from heat. Line a sheet pan with a silicone mat. Carefully drizzle the caramel onto the mat in long strings. Let cool and break into long shards.

To serve the dessert: portion the bread pudding into 4 x 2-inch rectangles. Spoon some of the chutney on each plate, top with a bread pudding rectangle. Drizzle the crème anglaise over the top and garnish with whipped cream, mint leaves, and a caramel shard.

MAKES 6 SERVINGS

FOR THE PRALINES

1 cup raw pecan halves
1 cup warm water
2 tablespoons powdered sugar
1/8 teaspoon salt

FOR THE CRUST

4 tablespoons butter
1 tablespoon sugar
Pinch of salt
3/4 cup flour
2 tablespoons cold water

FOR THE FILLING

2 medium sweet potatoes
2 eggs
1 egg yolk
4 tablespoons butter, melted
2 tablespoons brown sugar
2 tablespoons maple syrup
1/3 cup heavy cream
1 vanilla bean, split and scraped
1/4 teaspoon salt
1/4 teaspoon cinnamon
1/4 teaspoon cloves
1/4 teaspoon nutmeg

FOR THE GANACHE

3/4 cup heavy cream
1/2 cup chopped chocolate

SWEET POTATO PIE
with Chocolate Ganache and Pecan Pralines

A sweet, creamy pie filling is made with baked sweet potatoes and maple syrup, and topped with a smooth chocolate ganache—a splendid substitute for traditional pumpkin pie!

To prepare the pralines: preheat the oven to 290 degrees F. Add pecans to warm water and soak for 1 minute. Drain completely on paper towels, then toss the pecans in powdered sugar mixed with salt in a small bowl. Spoon onto a baking sheet in a single layer, and bake for 40 minutes, turning periodically. Remove from heat and let air-dry on the pan.

To prepare the crust: preheat the oven to 350 degrees F. In an electric mixer using the whip attachment, combine the butter, sugar, salt, and flour. Process until pea-size balls form. Slowly add the cold water until the dough pulls together. Wrap the dough in plastic wrap and refrigerate for 1 hour. On a flat, floured surface, roll the dough to 1/8 inch thickness. Line 6 (4-inch) tartlet pans with the dough and trim the edges. Poke holes in the bottom of each pie crust and bake them for just 8 minutes; this "blind" baking step sets the crust so the filling can be added. Let cool to room temperature.

To prepare the filling: preheat the oven to 425 degrees F. Place potatoes on a foil-lined pan; bake 45 to 60 minutes, or until tender. Peel when cool enough to handle and then purée in a food processor. Measure out 1 cup of purée; use any remaining purée for another purpose. In a metal mixing bowl, use a wire whisk to combine the eggs, egg yolk, and butter with the purée. Add the remaining ingredients to the mixture. Fill the baked tartlet pans with equal parts of the potato mixture and bake for 30 minutes; remove from oven and let cool for 15 minutes.

To prepare the ganache: scald the cream, in a medium saucepan over medium-high heat. Add the chocolate and remove from the heat. Let stand for 4 minutes and then whisk until smooth; set aside and keep warm.

To serve the dessert: remove the baked pies from the tartlet pans. Cover each tartlet with a thin layer of ganache. Top the pies with a pecan praline.

WINTER WELCOMES

January

The fir stands waist-deep in the bedded snow;

The storm-birds twitter, and in dark array

The broken peaks in shadow stand—when slow

The sun makes for a space all-blinding day,

While brown deer shyly track their silent way,

Hoof-patterning the snow-drifts as they go.

Maynard Dixon, 1896

WINTER IS THE CRESCENDO of Jackson Hole seasons, the longest and most dramatic. Although winter officially begins in December, snow can fall in Jackson as early as September and make surprise appearances through June. It can begin softly, with a freezing rain that be-

comes snowflakes, or it can roar into town with a whiteout blizzard. The first sign of winter appears with the white-capped mountain peaks, then makes its way to the valley floor. Although people often imagine Jackson Hole with arctic subzero temperatures, average winter temperatures range from 28 degrees F in December to 38 degrees F in March.

A popular Jackson bumper sticker says, "If you don't like snow, go home." No wonder then that Jackson offers a range of winter activities, from backcountry skiing to mushing through mountains on a dog sled.

True ski fanatics have their skis tuned and ready by Labor Day, anticipating that first day of untracked backcountry powder. Meanwhile, downhill fans mark the days until the opening of Jackson Hole Mountain Resort—one of the year's biggest events—heralding the official start of ski season. For the Nordic skier, it takes only enough snow to cover the

trails in Grand Teton National Park to create an ideal ski experience in one of the most spectacular settings.

But it's not necessary to ski to enjoy the beauty of winter here. From sleigh rides through the National Elk Refuge to snow coach adventures into Yellowstone National Park to snowshoe outings led by naturalists in Grand Teton National Park—all that's required is an interest in the outdoors and a warm coat and boots.

Jackson turns festive for the winter holiday season as the antler arches on the Town Square are bedazzled with twinkling lights, transforming into a magical venue for Santa as he arrives by sled dog team to listen to children's wishes for new skis and snowboards. One of Jackson's largest winter events is the Jackson Hole Winter Carnival in January. The annual event brings a variety of activities to town, from artist "quick-draws" and film festivals at the National Museum of Wildlife Art to the cornerstone event, the International Pedigree Stage Stop Sled Dog Race.

Photo credit: Tristan Greszko/JHMR

Jackson Hole Mountain Resort

Located at Teton Village, twelve miles northwest of Jackson, Jackson Hole Mountain Resort officially opened in 1966 and is considered by some to be simply the greatest ski area in North America. It includes two mountains within the beautiful Grand Teton mountain range and 2,500 acres of inbound terrain with a vertical drop of 4,139 feet—the greatest continuous rise in the U.S. The runs are 50 percent expert runs, 40 percent intermediate and 10 percent beginner. In addition to the massive amount of skiable inbound terrain, there is an even larger area to be explored "off piste," or out-of-bounds. Jackson Hole is home to many of the world's best freeskiers, with terrain considered to be some of the most challenging in North America and the world. The resort is known for short lift lines, outstanding views, and western hospitality; it is open December through April.

Photo credit: Tristan Greszko/JHMR

International Pedigree Stage Stop Sled Dog Race
Go, Dog, Go!

Each year on the last weekend of January, the fur flies in Jackson when the International Pedigree Stage Stop Sled Dog Race (IPSSSDR) comes to town. The largest sled dog race in

Photo credit: Morris Weintraub

the lower 48 states begins in Jackson before continuing to ten Wyoming towns over the next eight days. The town of Jackson "puts on the dog" when it hosts the first stage of the race, beginning with live music and a pig roast before the evening race through the town's streets to a torchlit parade and fireworks finale at Snow King Mountain. Known as the dog-friendly race because of its stage-stop format, which allows teams to rest overnight in the towns along the route, the IPSSSDR was founded by Iditarod musher Frank Teasley in 1996 and regularly attracts such sled-dog-racing greats as Doug Swingley, Jacques Philip, and Melanie Shirilla. Spectators need only bundle up for the formidably frosty fun and prepare to quaff cocoa as they catch the paw-pounding action.

Holidays at the Rusty Parrot

Holidays sparkle at the Rusty Parrot Lodge, when the inn is arrayed in beautiful decorations and tiny white lights. Owner Sandy Harrison chooses the ornaments that adorn a large Christmas tree in the front lobby, featuring hand-blown glass balls in natural tones of browns, greens, and reds contrasting with nature-themed ornaments and garlands. The staff also decorates a Christmas tree for the large guest suite of the lodge, and guests in other rooms can also request miniature Norfolk pines with lights during the holidays.

Garlands of natural pine are wound around the stair railings and placed on the fireplace mantel, intertwined with strings of cranberries and brightly colored ribbons. The staff decks the lodge for the holidays early in the week of Thanksgiving, when the Wild Sage cooks begin preparing a special Thanksgiving dinner that offers updated preparations of the traditional meal, like apple cider–brined roast turkey, cornbread stuffing, apple pie, and a decadent pumpkin-chocolate tart.

Christmas Eve is the busiest night of the holiday season, when guests partake of a special meal in the Wild Sage dining room. The menu might include temptations like beef tenderloin, lobster tail, duck, or a seafood-rich bouillabaisse; and the chefs also prepare several festive holiday desserts. When they return to their rooms, guests at the lodge are delighted to discover that St. Nicholas visited while they were out: a package of just-baked cookies hangs on their doors and specially chosen, wrapped Christmas presents await on their pillows—secretly placed by Santa's helpers during the nightly turn-down service.

The final celebration of the holiday season is a festive New Year's Eve menu at the Wild Sage, when champagne is poured during the second seating and revelers toast to all good things for the coming year.

A crackling wood fire blazes in the warm gathering room of the Wild Sage, where the winter menu offers substantial hearty fare to fuel cold-weather sports and activities. Soul-soothing soups, stews, and bisques are especially welcome when the snow flies just outside the big picture windows. Winter pears, cheeses, nuts, and root vegetables add texture and crunch to cool-weather salads, while appetizers might feature game like a tender venison loin accompanied by a Bing cherry compote, or a tender sage-stuffed squab breast.

Pork and beef are popular entrées, especially when accompanied by "comfort" side dishes like a crispy fennel and ham potato hash or spicy green beans—and the restaurant procures a surprising offering of fresh fish, flown in even during winter months. But the piece de resistance on the menu is often dessert; who can resist a sweet ending to a meal on a cold winter's night, especially if it's accompanied by a hot cup of espresso or a snifter of brandy? The Wild Sage's trademark "s'more" features a Grand Marnier–spiked brownie topped with a house-made orange blossom marshmallow and crispy graham cracker nougatine; diners may never settle for the plain version of the classic campfire treat again.

MAKES 4 TO 6 SERVINGS

1/2 cup unsalted butter

2 carrots, peeled and diced
   (1/4-inch cubes)

1 parsnip, peeled and diced
   (1/4-inch cubes)

1 white onion, diced (1/4-inch
   cubes)

2 cloves garlic, finely minced

6 celery ribs, diced (1/4-inch cubes)

1 pound elk short loin, cut into
   1/2-inch cubes

4 tablespoons flour

1 cup black barley

1 cup Burgundy or other dry
   red wine

1 quart veal stock

2 cups tomato juice

2 cups oyster mushrooms, cleaned
   and stems removed

1 rosemary sprig

2 thyme sprigs

1/2 teaspoon salt

1 teaspoon freshly ground black
   pepper

ELK AND BLACK BARLEY STEW

Rich and hearty, this soup combines root vegetables, elk short loin, wild mushrooms, and black barley. One of the only grains that can go from field to table without being processed, the barley lends a rustic, slightly chewy texture to the stew.

To prepare and serve the stew: Over medium heat in a large saucepan, melt the butter and sauté the carrots, parsnip, onion, garlic, and celery for 10 minutes. Dredge the elk cubes in flour and add to the pan. Cook for 4 minutes to form a roux, then add the barley. Deglaze the pan with wine, add the veal stock and tomato juice, and simmer for 25 minutes, or until barley is tender. Add the mushrooms, rosemary, and thyme, and cook for 10 minutes; remove rosemary and thyme from the pan. Season with salt and pepper and serve.

MAKES 6 TO 8 SERVINGS

FOR THE CROUTONS

3 tablespoons butter

2 teaspoons white truffle oil

2 cups diced crustless challah bread
(1/2-inch cubes)

FOR THE SOUP

2 (12-ounce) bottles Snake River
Lager or any style Vienna lager

6 cloves garlic

1 parsnip, peeled and diced (large
cubes)

1 carrot, peeled and diced (large
cubes)

3 shallots, peeled and roughly
chopped

2 cups heavy cream

2 cups chicken stock

1 pound Double Gloucester cheese,
hand-grated

2 tablespoons cornstarch

Salt, to taste

1/4 teaspoon ground white pepper

FOR THE GARNISH

12-year balsamic vinegar

SNAKE RIVER LAGER AND DOUBLE GLOUCESTER BÉCHAMEL SOUP
with Truffled Challah Croutons and 12-Year Balsamic Vinegar

A rich creamy soup gets its rustic flavor from lager
beer and Gloucester cheese, and a dash of aged
balsamic vinegar provides acidity.

To prepare the croutons: preheat the oven to 350 degrees F.
Heat a small sauté pan over medium-high heat and melt
the butter with the truffle oil. Toss the challah cubes with
the oil mixture and coat evenly. Spread the cubes on a
baking sheet and bake for 10 to 14 minutes, turning once,
until crisp and golden.

To prepare the soup: combine the beer, garlic, parsnip,
carrot, and shallots in a large saucepan and cook over
medium-high heat until reduced by half. Add the cream
and stock. Bring to a simmer for 10 minutes, remove from
heat, and strain back into the saucepan. Toss the cheese in
the cornstarch in a medium bowl, coating all surfaces. Add
the cheese mixture to the soup and bring back to a simmer;
do not boil. Add the salt and pepper, and stir.

To serve the soup: ladle into warmed soup bowls; top
with warm croutons and a few good dashes of aged
balsamic vinegar.

FOR THE BEETS

4 golden beets
1 tablespoon canola oil
1/4 teaspoon salt
1/4 teaspoon black pepper

FOR THE VINAIGRETTE

1/2 cup Verjus Blanc
1 teaspoon Dijon mustard
1/2 teaspoon pumpkin oil, divided
2 cloves garlic, peeled and minced
1 shallot, peeled and diced
1 tablespoon sugar
1/4 teaspoon salt
Pinch of freshly ground
    white pepper
2/3 cup grapeseed oil

FOR THE REDUCTION

1 cup Verjus Rouge
1/2 cup sugar

FOR THE GARNISH

Canola oil for frying
1 golden beet, peeled and thinly cut
    into shoestrings on a
    mandoline
Roasted pepitas

FOR THE ASPARAGUS

36 asparagus spears
1 tablespoon grapeseed oil
Pinch of salt
Pinch of freshly ground black
    pepper
2 ounces Point Reyes Blue Cheese

WARM ASPARAGUS AND BABY BEETS

with Point Reyes Blue Cheese, Verjus Rouge Gastrique, and Pumpkin Oil

Beets are slow-roasted to bring out their natural sweetness, layered with tangy blue cheese, and accompanied by tender fresh asparagus in this stacked salad. Both white and red verjus—the tart unfermented juice of unripe wine grapes— are used in a house-made vinaigrette and as a sweet reduction to accompany the salad.

To prepare the beets: preheat the oven to 300 degrees F. Coat beets with oil, salt, and pepper; wrap tightly in foil and roast for 2-1/2 hours, or until easily pierced with a knife. Let cool until warm, then remove foil and rub skin off the beets with a clean kitchen towel. Cut the beets into 1/4-inch slices. Cut the slices into perfect rounds with a round cookie cutter; set aside.

To prepare the vinaigrette: combine all the ingredients except the oil. Process slowly, emulsifying the oil into the verjus; strain. Set aside and keep cold.

To prepare the reduction: place both ingredients in a small saucepan and reduce to about 2/3 cup over medium-high heat. Small syrupy bubbles will form after about 12 minutes. Cool and then transfer to a plastic squeeze bottle. Keep at room temperature.

To prepare the garnish: heat the oil to 320 degrees F and fry the beet shoestrings until the oil stops bubbling; drain on a tray lined with paper towels in a single layer and let air-dry and crisp for at least 1 hour.

To prepare the asparagus: toss asparagus with oil, salt, and pepper, and roast for about 8 minutes. Layer beets with a very thin layer of blue cheese, making a stack of 4–5 slices; roast at 350 degrees F for 8 minutes. After the beets and asparagus are finished, drizzle with the vinaigrette.

To serve the salad: use 6 spears of asparagus and one beet stack per plate. Drizzle with verjus reduction and sprinkle the pepitas on the plate.

FOR THE PEARS

2 cups Pinot Noir

2 cinnamon sticks

1 cup sugar

4 cups cold water

1 vanilla bean, split

3 D'Anjou pears, peeled and cored

FOR THE VINAIGRETTE

2 tablespoons Pommery
    mustard

1 egg

1/2 cup champagne vinegar

1/2 teaspoon salt

1 tablespoon sugar

1/8 teaspoon freshly ground white
    pepper

1 clove garlic, peeled and minced

1/2 shallot, peeled and minced

1 tablespoon walnut oil

1 cup canola oil

FOR THE WALNUTS

1 cup walnut halves

1 cup warm water

1/4 cup powdered sugar

1/8 teaspoon salt

FOR THE SALAD

3 heads curly endive, washed,
    dried, and trimmed

1 head Belgian endive, washed
    and julienned

FOR THE GARNISH:

3 tablespoons crumbled lemon
    Stilton cheese

CURLY ENDIVE
with Pommery Mustard Vinaigrette,
Burgundy-Poached Pears, Lemon Stilton,
and Candied Walnuts

A sophisticated salad combines endive, pears gently poached
in Pinot Noir, and a homemade mustard-based vinaigrette.
The salad is topped with lemon Stilton, a cheese variety that
contains lemon peel, giving the soft cheese a dimensional
texture and slightly sweeter flavor.

To prepare the pears: reduce the wine in a tall-sided saucepan over high heat and cook off the alcohol. Add the remaining ingredients to the liquid and cover with a coffee filter. Cook the mixture until it comes to a boil. Remove from the heat and refrigerate the pears in the liquid overnight.

To prepare the vinaigrette: combine all the ingredients except oils and process in a blender until smooth. Slowly emulsify the oils into mixture; strain and reserve in the refrigerator.

To prepare the walnuts: preheat the oven to 290 degrees F. In a small bowl, combine walnuts with warm water and soak for 1 minute. Drain completely and then toss in a mixture of powdered sugar and salt. Bake for 40 minutes, turning periodically. Let air-dry on oven sheet pan.

To serve the salad: in a large mixing bowl use enough vinaigrette to coat all the leaves of the endives evenly. Place dressed greens in the center of each plate. Slice each pear into six equal portions; encircle the greens with 3 pieces of pear. Top the greens with walnut halves and cheese.

MAKES 4 TO 6 SERVINGS

FOR THE GARNISH

1/2 pound pancetta

FOR THE VINAIGRETTE

2 shallots, peeled
2 cloves garlic, peeled
1 cup canola oil
1/2 cup sherry vinegar
1/4 cup brown sugar
1/2 teaspoon salt
1 tablespoon Dijon mustard

FOR THE CONFIT

1 red bell pepper
3 cloves garlic
1 thyme sprig
1-1/2 cups olive oil

FOR THE GOAT CHEESE

1/2 pound Humbolt Fog
    goat cheese, rind removed
1 tablespoon chopped fresh
    thyme leaves
2 eggs, beaten
3 tablespoons flour
1 cup crushed corn flakes
1 cup canola oil

FOR THE SALAD

2 heads frisée, washed and dried

GRIDDLED HAYSTACK MOUNTAIN GOAT CHEESE
with Frisée, Brown Sugar–Roasted Shallot Vinaigrette, Pancetta, and Red Pepper Confit

Curly frisée is paired with a crispy fried round of creamy goat cheese and accompanied by a house-made Dijon dressing; the Wild Sage chefs create the ultimate "bacon bits"—crunchy Italian pancetta—to top the colorful salad.

To prepare the garnish: preheat the oven to 350 degrees F. Slice the pancetta into 1/8-inch slices. Place the slices on a parchment-lined sheet tray. Top the slices with another sheet of parchment and a second sheet tray to keep the pancetta flat while cooking. Cook for about 12–15 minutes, or until completely rendered and crisp. Cool on a tray lined with paper towels.

To prepare the vinaigrette: preheat the oven to 350 degrees F. In a small ovenproof dish, roast the shallots and garlic in the oil for 45 minutes; cool, strain out the oil, and reserve. Process the shallots and garlic in a blender with the remaining ingredients; slowly add the reserved oil until it is emulsified into the mixture.

To prepare the confit: preheat the oven to 300 degrees F. Remove all seeds and veins from the pepper. Cut into quarters, place all items in a small ovenproof container, and roast for 1-1/4 hours. Let cool, peel the skin, and brunoise the meat of the pepper; set aside and keep warm.

To prepare the goat cheese: bring cheese to room temperature and fold in the fresh thyme. Portion and mold the cheese into small 1-1/2- to 2-ounce rounds (3 or 4 tablespoons each). Dip goat cheese into the egg, dredge with flour, and roll in corn flakes. Heat the oil in a pan over medium heat. Working in batches, sear the goat cheese on both sides for about 1 minute per side, or until golden brown. Remove and let rest on a plate lined with paper towels.

To serve the salad: spoon some of the confit in a circle on the plate and top with the warm griddled goat cheese. Place one piece of rendered pancetta on the goat cheese. Toss the frisée in the vinaigrette and arrange on top of the pancetta.

FOR THE COMPOTE

1/2 cup dried Bing cherries
1 cup warm water
1/2 cup Tempranillo wine
2 tablespoons sugar
1 tablespoon balsamic vinegar

FOR THE CHIPS

Canola oil
1 celery root, sliced paper thin on a
  slicer or mandolin
Salt to taste

FOR THE PURÉE

1 quart water
1 teaspoon salt
1 celery root, peeled and diced (1/2-
  inch cubes, should yield about 2
  cups)
2 ounces white chocolate, melted
1/8 teaspoon salt

FOR THE VENISON

2 tablespoons finely
  ground espresso
2 tablespoons cocoa
1 pound venison short loin, cut into
  6 portions
1 teaspoon salt
2 tablespoons canola oil

ESPRESSO- AND COCOA-DUSTED VENISON LOIN

with Bing Cherry Compote and Celery Knob Purée

It sounds unusual, but a dusting of cocoa and espresso perfectly balances the hearty venison, which is accompanied by a purée of celery root that gets just a hint of sweetness from white chocolate. The dish is finished with a tangy dried-cherry compote.

To prepare the compote: cover the cherries with warm water in a small bowl and let hydrate for 30 minutes. Add the wine, sugar, vinegar, cherries, and soaking water to a small saucepan. Cook over medium-high heat until the liquid is reduced by 60 percent; set aside and keep warm.

To prepare the chips: heat the oil in a fryer or tall-sided pot to 300 degrees F. Fry the celery root slices until lightly golden and the oil stops bubbling. Drain on a tray lined with paper towels; sprinkle with salt and let crisp for at least 1 hour.

To prepare the purée: heat the water and salt to boiling in a medium pot and cook the diced celery root in the water for about 24 minutes, or until tender. Process in a food processor until creamy and smooth. Add the white chocolate while warm to emulsify into the celery root mixture; add the salt. Set aside and keep warm.

To prepare the venison: combine the espresso and cocoa, and mix well. Lightly dust each portion of venison and season with salt. Preheat the oven to 350 degrees F. In a sauté pan over medium heat, sear the venison in the canola oil to set the crust, about 15–20 seconds on each side (take care not to burn the crust). Transfer the venison to a baking pan and finish in the oven for 4–5 minutes, then remove to a wire rack and let rest for 5 minutes.

To serve the appetizer: slice the venison on the bias and plate on top of the compote and around the purée. Garnish with celery root chips. Makes 6 servings.

Wine Pairing Pascual Toso Cabernet Sauvignon, Mendoza, Argentina

Tasting Notes This wine accentuates the light gaminess of the venison and pairs well with the espresso and cocoa components of the dish.

MAKES 6 SERVINGS

FOR THE STOCK

1/2 pound hon shemeji mushrooms

1-1/2 cups water

1/2 cup diced celery (1/2-inch cubes)

1/2 cup diced carrot (1/2-inch cubes)

3 cloves garlic, peeled

1 shallot, peeled and sliced

1 bay leaf

1 sprig rosemary

FOR THE GNUDI

2 cups ricotta cheese

2 eggs

4 tablespoons grated
    Grana Padano cheese

2 tablespoons fresh sage chiffonade

1/2 teaspoon salt

1 cup flour

1 quart water

1 teaspoon salt

FOR THE BROWN BUTTER

1/2 cup butter

FOR THE RAGOUT

2 tablespoons olive oil

1 garlic clove, brunoised

1 shallot, brunoised

1/2 teaspoon salt

1-1/2 teaspoons fresh
    thyme leaves

FOR THE SPECK

2 ounces trimmed speck ham

FOR THE GARNISH

6 fresh sage leaves

Canola oil

GNUDI
with Sage and Brown Butter, Hon Shemeji Mushroom Ragout, and Crispy Speck Ham

Gnudi are best described as ravioli filling without the pasta.
Here, the tender ricotta-based dumplings are served with
an earthy wild mushroom ragout and topped with nutty
browned butter and crispy ham.

To prepare the stock: trim the mushrooms to a 1-inch length, save the trimmed bases, and set aside the tops for the ragout. In a medium saucepan, combine the water, mushroom bases, celery, carrot, garlic, shallot, and bay leaf. Simmer the mixture over medium heat until the liquid is reduced by two-thirds. Add the rosemary for the last 2 minutes of cooking. Strain the mixture and discard the solids; set aside.

To prepare the gnudi: combine the ricotta, eggs, cheese, sage, and salt in a mixing bowl. Sift the flour into the mixture and fold in with a rubber spatula. Do not over-mix. Chill the mixture for 1 hour.

Make an ice bath. In a medium saucepan, heat the water and salt to a boil. Form the ricotta mixture into quenelles and place in the boiling water. When they float, they are done. Remove from the water and place in the ice bath. Once the gnudi are fully cooled, remove from the ice bath and reserve on a tray lined with paper towels.

To prepare the brown butter: heat the butter over low heat in a small saucepan. Remove from the heat when the solids fall to the bottom of the pan and begin to brown. Gently transfer the butter to another container and strain; discard the solids.

To prepare the ragout: heat the oil in a large sauté pan over medium-high heat until almost smoking. Cook the mushroom tops and caramelize on one side. Add the garlic and shallot. Deglaze with the mushroom stock. Reduce the mixture by half, remove from the heat, and add the salt and thyme.

To prepare the speck: preheat the oven to 300 degrees F. Cut the speck into 1/2-inch julienne. Arrange on a baking sheet and bake for 20 minutes. Remove from oven and cool to room temperature.

To prepare the garnish: heat one inch of vegetable oil in a small saucepan until it registers 365 degrees F on a deep-fat thermometer. Drop the sage leaves in the hot oil and fry just until crisp, about 3 to 5 seconds. Transfer leaves with a slotted spoon to paper towels to drain.

To serve the appetizer: heat the brown butter in a sauté pan and sear the gnudi until golden brown on all sides. Spoon some of the warm ragout on each plate and top with the gnudi. Garnish with the speck ham and sage leaves.

Wine Pairing Long Shadows Pedestal Merlot, Columbia Valley, Washington

Tasting Notes This dish has tremendous richness with the goat cheese in the gnudi, the brown butter, the earthiness of the ragout, and the fat of the speck ham. To complement these elements, this wine exhibits some forward fruit characteristics and great depth.

MAKES 6 SERVINGS

FOR THE POLENTA

1-1/2 cups chicken stock
1/2 cup polenta
1/3 cup heavy cream
1/4 teaspoon salt
1/8 teaspoon white pepper
2 ounces white truffle cheese, such
   as Boschetto al Tartufo, grated

FOR THE "PAINT"

1 cup ruby port
2 tablespoons sugar

FOR THE ARUGULA

1-1/2 cups canola oil
36 fresh arugula leaves
1/2 teaspoon kosher salt

FOR THE SQUAB

3 whole squabs
12 fresh sage leaves
1/4 teaspoon salt
1/4 teaspoon pepper
2 tablespoons olive oil

SAGE-STUFFED SQUAB BREAST
with White Truffle Polenta Cake, Fried Arugula, and Port Wine "Paint"

Sage leaves are gently tucked under the breast of tender squab, imparting a delicate flavor to the meat. The dish is accompanied by a cake of creamy polenta flavored with an aromatic white truffle cheese.

To prepare the polenta: bring the stock to a boil in a small saucepan over medium-high heat and then add the polenta. Cook over low heat for 15 minutes, constantly stirring. Add the remaining ingredients, stir just until combined, and then immediately remove from the heat; set aside and keep warm.

To prepare the "paint": combine the port and sugar in a small saucepan over medium-high heat and cook until the mixture is syrupy and reduced to about 1/2 cup; set aside and keep warm.

To prepare the arugula: heat a small tall-sided saucepan with the canola oil to 375 degrees F. Carefully drop single leaves of arugula in the oil (the moisture in the arugula may cause the oil to pop) for 30 seconds, then dry on a platter lined with paper towels and sprinkle with salt.

To prepare the squab: remove the breast and legs from the bird. Trim the breast of all sinew and place two sage leaves under the skin of each breast. The legs should be trimmed at the top of the bone and pushed down to create a "lollipop."

In the same oil used for preparing the arugula, cook the squab legs for 2 minutes, or until golden brown; drain. Sprinkle with salt and pepper; set aside and keep warm.

Heat the olive oil in a sauté pan over high heat. Season the squab breasts with salt and pepper, and sauté them, fat-side-first, for about 1-1/2 minutes, until golden; turn over and sear for 1 minute more. The squab should be medium-rare.

To serve the appetizer: slice the squab on a bias. Using two spoons, form quenelles of the polenta and place one on each plate. Place a piece of squab on the polenta, drizzle or use a brush to paint the port wine syrup on the plate, and garnish with fried arugula.

Wine Pairing **Mauro Molino Barolo La Morra, Piedmont, Italy**

Tasting Notes **Truffles and Barolo make everyone happy!**

MAKES 6 SERVINGS

FOR THE JAM

1/2 cup sugar
1/2 cup water
Juice of 1/2 lemon
1/2 cup diced fresh horseradish root
  (large cubes)
5 Roma tomatoes

FOR THE FONDUE

2 leeks, white and tender green
  parts only, cut in 1/4-inch dice
1 tablespoon canola oil
1 (5.2-ounce) round Boursin cheese
1/2 pound Neufchâtel cheese

FOR THE HASH

18 fingerling potatoes
3 tablespoons canola oil, divided
1 teaspoon salt
1 teaspoon freshly ground black
  pepper
1/4 pound speck ham, crusty edge
  removed and diced (1/4-inch
  cubes)
1 white onion
1 fennel bulb, peeled and diced
  (1/4-inch cubes, about 1 cup)
1 tablespoon fresh thyme leaves

MONTANA BEEF TENDERLOIN
with Boursin and Leek Fondue,
Tomato-Horseradish Jam, Speck Ham,
and Fennel Potato Hash

Beef tenderloin is cooked to perfection and topped with a
creamy sauce of Boursin cheese and leeks. The crispy fennel
potato hash recipe can be doubled or tripled and prepared as a
stand-alone side dish.

FOR THE TENDERLOINS

6 (8-ounce) center-cut Montana
  legend beef tenderloins
1 tablespoon salt
1-1/2 teaspoons freshly ground
  black pepper
2 tablespoons canola oil

FOR THE GARNISH

6 slices prosciutto
18 asparagus spears, trimmed and
  blanched

To prepare the jam: place the sugar, water, lemon juice, and horseradish root in a small saucepan. Reduce until it thickens to syrup. In a large saucepan, bring 2 quarts of water to a boil. Add tomatoes to the water and cook for 30 seconds. Shock tomatoes in an ice bath and then peel the skin; fillet the tomatoes lengthwise, discarding all the seeds. Add to syrup and cook for 10 minutes until syrup consistency is regained. Use a slotted spoon to remove the horseradish pieces and discard. Cool the jam to room temperature.

To prepare the fondue: soak the chopped leeks in cold water to remove any dirt and debris; drain thoroughly. In a sauté pan, add the oil and sweat the leeks over low heat. Remove from heat and cool to room temperature; fold leeks into combined cheeses in a medium bowl and set aside.

To prepare the hash: preheat the oven to 350 degrees F. Slice the potatoes on the bias into a medium bowl and toss in 2 tablespoons oil; season with salt and pepper. Spoon into a baking pan and roast until tender, about 30 minutes. In a large sauté pan, cook the ham in the remaining oil for about 5 minutes over high heat. Add the onion and fennel, and cook until tender and translucent. Keep warm and toss with roasted potatoes when they come out of the oven. Set aside and keep warm; when ready to serve, mix in the fresh thyme.

To prepare the tenderloins: preheat the oven to 400 degrees F. Bring the steaks to room temperature and season with salt and pepper. Heat the canola oil in a sauté pan over high heat and sear the tenderloin on both flat sides. Move the steaks to a baking pan and finish in the oven for about 4 minutes. Take steaks out of the oven and top with the fondue; return to the oven for 4–6 minutes until medium-rare. Remove from the oven and let rest for 5 minutes.

To serve the entrée: place the potato hash in the center of each plate. Top with the tenderloin and spoon some of the fondue on top. Pour some of the tomato jam on the plate next to the tenderloin. Wrap each piece of prosciutto around three asparagus spears and lean against the steak to garnish.

Wine Pairing suggestion: Clos du Val "Oak Vineyard" Cabernet, Stag's Leap District, Napa Valley, California

Tasting Notes A balanced, full-bodied Cabernet pairs well with this elegant beef preparation.

MAKES 5 SERVINGS

FOR THE SPICE CRUST MIXTURE

1 tablespoon mustard seeds

2 tablespoons coriander seeds

FOR THE CHUTNEY

1 mango, diced (1/4-inch cubes)

1 cup water

1 tablespoon Banyuls vinegar

2 tablespoons sugar

FOR THE SALAD

1 English cucumber, peeled

1 red onion

1/2 tablespoon lemon juice

1 tablespoon Banyuls vinegar

1/2 teaspoon salt

1 tablespoon extra virgin olive oil

1 tablespoon chopped flat-leaf
    parsley

MUSTARD- AND CORIANDER-CRUSTED WILD ALASKAN HALIBUT
with Whipped Potato Samosa, Mango Chutney, and Cucumber Salad

Crushed mustard and coriander seeds create a spicy crust for mild, flaky halibut. The Wild Sage kitchen prepares crispy potato samosas, a popular oft-requested side dish, to accompany the fish.

FOR THE SAMOSAS

4 medium Yukon gold
    potatoes, scrubbed

4 cups canola oil, divided

1/2 cup peeled and diced
    carrots (1/4-inch cubes)

1/2 large red onion, peeled
    and diced (1/4-inch cubes)

1 tablespoon minced fresh garlic

1/2 cup shelled sweet peas

1 tablespoon fresh ginger
    brunoise

1/3 cup heavy cream

4 tablespoons butter

1 tablespoon Madras curry pow-
    der

5 sheets feuille de brick
    or egg roll wrappers

1/2 teaspoon kosher salt

FOR THE HALIBUT

5 (6-ounce) wild Alaskan
    halibut fillets

1 teaspoon salt

1 teaspoon ground white pepper

3 tablespoons grapeseed oil

To prepare the spice crust mixture: combine and grind the mustard and coriander seeds in a spice grinder.

To prepare the chutney: combine all the ingredients in a saucepan. Cook the mixture over low heat until it thickens and becomes slightly syrupy; set aside and keep warm.

To prepare the salad: julienne the cucumber into fine strands on a mandoline, about the thickness of spaghetti. Do not use the seedy center of the cucumber. Julienne the onion and mix with the cucumber. Combine the lemon juice, vinegar, and salt in a small bowl. Whisk in the oil until the mixture is emulsified, and then fold in the parsley. Gently stir the dressing into the cucumber-onion mixture; chill.

To prepare the samosas: place the potatoes in a large pot, add enough cold water to cover by 2 inches, and bring to a boil over high heat. Cook until the potatoes are tender when pierced with the tip of a sharp knife. Drain the potatoes on a towel until cool enough to handle. Peel the warm potatoes and then put them through a potato ricer into a large bowl.

Heat a large sauté pan over medium heat and add 2 tablespoons of the oil. Sauté the carrots and onion, stirring occasionally, until tender. Add the garlic, peas, and ginger, and cook 5 minutes more. Remove from the heat and add the vegetable mixture to the riced potatoes.

In a small saucepan, heat the cream, butter, and curry powder just until simmering; don't let it boil. Remove from the heat and fold the cream mixture into the potatoes. Cool the potato mixture in the refrigerator for 2 hours.

In a medium, tall-sided saucepan, heat the remaining oil to 350 degrees F. Roll the potato mixture into cigar shapes approximately 3/4 inch in diameter and 4 inches long. Lay out a sheet of feuille de brick or an egg roll wrapper and roll around the potato mixture. Wrap all the potatoes in the same fashion. Fry the samosas in the canola oil in batches until they are golden brown. Drain on a tray lined with paper towels and sprinkle with salt.

To prepare the halibut: preheat the oven to 350 degrees F. Coat the top of the halibut with the mustard and coriander spice mixture, and season with salt and pepper. Heat the oil in a large sauté pan over medium heat and sear the halibut, crust-side-down, until golden brown; turn the fillets and sear the other side. Finish the fish in the oven to desired doneness.

To serve the entrée: place a samosa in the center of each plate. Spoon some of the cucumber salad to the side, and then top with a halibut fillet. Garnish with a scoop of chutney.

Wine Pairing   Frederic Magnien Chassagne-Montrachet 1er Cru "La Maltroie," Burgundy, France

Tasting Notes This dish is well-suited to a white burgundy from one of the great domaines.

MAKES 6 SERVINGS

FOR THE RELISH

1 cup diced mango (1/2-inch cubes)

1 teaspoon rice wine vinegar

1 teaspoon lime juice

1/2 cup sugar

1 cup water

FOR THE BACON

2 pounds pork belly

1 cup tamari

1 large ginger lobe

5 cloves garlic, smashed

2 shallots, sliced 1/2-inch thick

3 cups water

FOR THE TENDERLOIN

2-1/4 pounds pork tenderloin
   (6-ounce portions)

2 cups canola oil

3 cloves garlic, halved

1 shallot, cut into 1/2-inch slices

1 thumb-size ginger lobe, peeled
   and chopped

1 bunch cilantro, roughly chopped

2 star anise pods

2 dried bird's-eye chiles

2 tablespoons canola oil, reserved
   for searing

FOR THE POTATOES

2 russet potatoes, peeled

2 cups sake

2 cloves garlic

1 shallot

1 cup chicken broth

1 teaspoon salt

TAMARI BACON–STRUNG PORK TENDERLOIN
with Sake Potato Parisienne and Spicy Haricots Verts

Homemade bacon is wrapped around individual

portions of pork tenderloin, adding an incredible

depth of flavor and moistness to the meat.

FOR THE GLAZE

1/2 cup tamari

1 cup water

1/4 cup sugar

3 teaspoons cornstarch

2 cloves garlic, peeled and
   smashed

1 ginger lobe, peeled and
   roughly chopped

1 shallot, peeled and sliced

1 teaspoon hot chile garlic sauce

2 teaspoons fish sauce

FOR THE HARICOTS VERTS

1 tablespoon canola oil

3/4 pound haricots verts, trimmed
   and blanched

1 red bell pepper, seeded and
   brunoised

3 ounces (about 1/3 cup) basil
   stems

3 ounces (about 1/3 cup) fresh
   basil chiffonade

1 quart water

1 teaspoon salt

3 serrano chiles, thinly sliced

To prepare the relish: combine all the ingredients in a small saucepan and cook over medium heat until the mixture is syrupy and reduced by half, about 2/3 cup; refrigerate until ready to use.

To prepare the bacon: place all the ingredients in the smallest pan possible that will hold them. Cure in the refrigerator for two days, turning twice per day. Remove the pork belly from the cure and pat dry. Turn on an electric smoker and fill with cherrywood chips; smoke the pork for 3 hours. Remove from smoker, wrap in plastic, and put in the freezer until partially frozen. Remove from freezer and slice with an electric knife into 1/8-inch slices; set aside.

To prepare the tenderloin: begin marinating the pork on the second day that the bacon is curing. Place the pork with all ingredients except reserved oil in a pot, cover, and let marinate in the refrigerator for two days. On the third day, remove pork from the marinade and pat dry. Wrap the slices of bacon around each tenderloin portion to cover all sides except the ends.

Preheat the oven to 400 degrees F. Heat the reserved oil in a large sauté pan over medium heat. Render all sides of the bacon-wrapped pork until brown and crisp. Transfer the pork to a baking sheet and finish in the oven to desired temperature (medium will take about 6 minutes).

To prepare the potatoes: make balls from the potatoes using a small melon baller and place in a bowl of water to prevent browning. (Discard or reserve hull of potato for another use.) In a tall-sided saucepan, combine the sake, garlic, and shallot, and cook over high heat until reduced by one-third. Add the broth, salt, and potato balls to the mixture and cook for 14 minutes, or until potatoes are just tender. Remove from the heat and let the potatoes rest in the cooking liquid until ready to plate.

To prepare the glaze: combine all ingredients except the fish sauce in a medium-size saucepan. Stir to mix well. Heat over medium-high heat until the mixture comes to a boil and thickens. Strain out all the solids and add the fish sauce; set aside and keep warm.

To prepare the haricots verts: heat the oil in a sauté pan over high heat. At the smoking point, add the haricots verts and cook for 1 minute. Add the bell pepper and basil stems, and sauté for 1 minute more. Remove pan from heat; add 6 tablespoons tamari glaze and the basil chiffonade. Bring up to temperature; set aside and keep warm.

To serve the entrée: 2 minutes before the pork is ready to come out of the oven, drizzle the tamari glaze over the individual portions of pork and return to the oven to set the glaze. Remove pork from the oven and let rest for 5 minutes, then slice on a bias in the middle. Place the haricots verts in the center of each plate and top with the tenderloin and some of the mango relish. Use a slotted spoon to remove the potatoes from the poaching liquid and arrange them in a circle around the pork and haricots verts.

Wine Pairing **Cims de Porrera Classic, Priorat, Catalunya, Spain**

Tasting Notes **The wine's smooth tannins and fresh acidity pair well with the richness of the tenderloin.**

MAKES 6 SERVINGS

FOR THE ICE CREAM

1/2 cup sugar

6 egg yolks

2 cups heavy cream

1 vanilla bean, split and scraped

3 tablespoons hyson green tea,
    wrapped in cheesecloth

FOR THE CHUTNEY

2 ounces jaggery

2 cups water

2 tablespoons peeled fresh ginger
    brunoise

3 Asian pears, cored and diced
    (about 2 cups)

FOR THE WAFFLES

1/2 cup buttermilk

1/2 cup half-and-half

3 eggs

1 tablespoon peeled ginger
    brunoise

1/4 teaspoon salt

1/2 cup sugar

1/2 cup buckwheat flour

1/2 cup flour

FOR THE GARNISH

Fresh lemongrass

BUCKWHEAT WAFFLES
with Jaggery Asian Pear Chutney and Green Tea Ice Cream

Not just for breakfast anymore, sweet waffles are served warm with a scoop of house-made vanilla ice cream that has a delicate green tea flavor; the topping is a warm compote made of fresh Asian pears and ginger.

To prepare the ice cream: set up a double boiler with a metal mixing bowl. Combine the sugar with the egg yolks and stir with a whisk until pale yellow and fluffy. Add the cream, vanilla, and tea packet, and cook in the double boiler until the mixture reaches 175 degrees F. Strain and discard the tea packet. Chill the mixture in the refrigerator for 4 hours and then process in an ice cream maker according to the manufacturer's directions. Transfer to a container and freeze overnight.

To prepare the chutney: combine the jaggery, water, and ginger in a tall-sided saucepan. Reduce by half over medium heat and then strain through a fine mesh sieve, discarding the ginger. Return the mixture to the heat, add the pears, and cook for 12 minutes, until thick and syrupy; set aside and keep warm.

To prepare the waffles: process the buttermilk, half-and-half, eggs, and ginger in a blender for 1 minute. Strain through a fine mesh sieve into a metal mixing bowl. Add the salt and sugar, and mix well. Sift the flours into the mixture to make the batter. Preheat the waffle iron. Portion the batter into the iron and cook according to manufacturer's directions.

To serve the dessert: top the waffle with the chutney and a quenelle of ice cream; garnish with a few sprigs of lemongrass.

FOR THE CRUST

1 cup crushed vanilla crème sand-
    wich cookies
1/2 cup chopped macadamia nuts
2 tablespoons melted butter

FOR THE CHEESECAKE

3 pounds cream cheese, room
    temperature
2 cups sugar
7 eggs
1/3 cup coffee liqueur (such as
    Kahlúa)
1 vanilla bean, split and scraped

FOR THE GANACHE

1 cup heavy cream
1 cup finely chopped semisweet
    dark chocolate

KAHLÚA CHEESECAKE
with Vanilla–Macadamia Nut Crust and Warm Chocolate Ganache

A decadent cheesecake is flavored with coffee liqueur and served atop a pool of smooth, creamy ganache. The crunchy crust is made with a surprising ingredient: old-fashioned vanilla crème sandwich cookies.

To prepare the crust: preheat a convection oven to 350 degrees F. In a food processor fitted with a metal blade, combine the cookies and nuts. Process until ground very finely. Slowly add the butter until the mixture looks slightly moist and holds its shape when compressed. Remove the mixture from the bowl and pack tightly into a 9-inch parchment-lined springform pan. Bake for 8 minutes, or until edges become slightly golden. Remove the pan from the oven and let cool to room temperature on a wire rack.

To prepare the cheesecake: preheat the oven to 295 degrees F. In a food processor fitted with a metal blade, combine the cream cheese and sugar until smooth (working in batches, if necessary). Add eggs, coffee liqueur, and vanilla bean to the mixture, and process until batter is extremely smooth and creamy. Strain the mixture through a fine mesh sieve to remove any clumps. Use sheets of aluminum foil to encompass the outside of the springform pan and create a watertight seal. Pour the batter into the prepared pan and bake for 4 hours in a water bath. The center should not appear liquid but should move as one when jiggled. Remove from the oven and refrigerate overnight in the pan.

To prepare the ganache: scald the cream in a saucepan. Add the chocolate to the scalded cream. Remove from the heat and let rest for 3 minutes. Using a wire whisk, mix until the chocolate is homogenous and smooth. Set aside and keep warm.

To serve the dessert: using a paring knife, free the edges of the cheesecake and remove the springform pan. Portion into 12 equal pieces. Arrange one slice in the center of each plate over a pool of the chocolate ganache.

MAKES 8 SERVINGS

FOR THE BROWNIES

1 cup chopped dark chocolate
1/2 cup plus 3 tablespoons butter
1 tablespoon Grand Marnier
1-1/8 cups sugar
2 eggs
Pinch of salt
1/2 teaspoon vanilla extract
1/2 cup flour

FOR THE MARSHMALLOWS

1 envelope (1 tablespoon)
   unflavored gelatin
1/2 cup cold water
1/2 cup sugar
2 tablespoons orange blossom
   honey
2 tablespoons brown sugar
1/2 cup light corn syrup
3 tablespoons hot water
1 egg white

FOR THE NOUGATINE

1/2 cup sugar
1/2 cup water
2/3 cup finely ground graham
   crackers

FOR THE COULIS

1 cup fresh-squeezed blood orange
   juice (about 6 oranges)
1/3 cup sugar
Pinch of salt

FOR THE GARNISH

Candied orange slice or zest

GRAND MARNIER CHOCOLATE BROWNIE
with Orange Blossom Marshmallow, Graham Cracker Nougatine, and Blood Orange Coulis

A grown-up version of s'mores, this is one of the restaurant's most popular desserts. The chefs prepare rich dark chocolate brownies enlivened with orange liqueur and top them with homemade marshmallows and a crispy graham-cracker-based nougatine.

To prepare the brownies: preheat the oven to 325 degrees F. Set up a double boiler with a metal mixing bowl. Melt the chocolate and butter in the double boiler with the Grand Marnier. Remove from heat and cool. Meanwhile, combine the sugar and eggs in a separate mixing bowl and whisk until pale yellow; then add salt and vanilla. Stir the chocolate mixture into the egg mixture until fully combined. Fold in the flour until just incorporated. Spread the batter on a parchment-lined 8 x 8-inch baking pan that has been coated with nonstick spray. Bake for 25 minutes, or until a toothpick comes out clean. Cool to room temperature.

To prepare the marshmallows: Soften the gelatin in the cold water. In a tall-sided saucepan over medium heat, combine the sugar, honey, brown sugar, corn syrup, and hot water, and heat to 240 degrees F. Remove from heat; stir in gelatin mixture to dissolve. Let cool 10 minutes. In a metal electric mixer bowl, beat the egg white to stiff peaks. Slowly drizzle the hot sugar mixture into the egg whites and increase the speed of mixer to high. Beat for about 8 minutes, or until the mixture is snow white and three times the original volume. Immediately spread the mixture on top of the brownies.

To prepare the nougatine: combine the sugar and water in a saucepan and cook over high heat until amber in color; remove from heat and stir in graham cracker crumbs. Pour on a baking sheet to cool (if any large lumps form, simply chop with a knife while mixture is still warm).

To prepare the coulis: combine all the ingredients in a saucepan and cook over medium heat until reduced by two-thirds (should yield about 1/2 cup).

To serve the dessert: use a 2-inch round biscuit cutter to cut the marshmallow-covered brownies into 16 rounds. Using a food-grade torch, lightly toast the marshmallow topping. Break up the nougatine and sprinkle it on top of 8 of the brownie rounds; top each with another brownie round and transfer to individual plates. Garnish each brownie with a candied orange slice or orange zest.

The Rusty Parrot's Legendary Cookies

A hallmark of a stay at the Rusty Parrot, freshly baked cookies are placed in the gathering room every afternoon for guests to enjoy with coffee or tea after returning from the day's activities. Here are several of the restaurant's most-requested cookie recipes.

MAKES 16 SERVINGS

3/4 cup packed brown sugar
1 egg
2 teaspoons vanilla extract
1/2 cup unsalted butter,
   melted
1-1/2 cups flour
1 teaspoon baking powder
1/8 teaspoon salt
1 cup roasted and chopped
   hazelnuts
1/2 cup chopped white
   chocolate

HAZELNUT AND WHITE CHOCOLATE BLONDIES

To prepare the blondies: preheat the oven to 350 degrees F. Butter and flour an 8 x 8-inch baking pan. Using an electric mixer, cream the sugar and egg; add the vanilla and butter. Sift in the flour, baking powder, and salt. Fold in hazelnuts and chocolate. Spread in prepared pan and bake for 25 to 30 minutes, rotating every 10 minutes. Let cool to room temperature and cut into 2-inch squares.

MAKES 2 DOZEN COOKIES

1 cup butter
3/4 cup sugar
3/4 cup brown sugar
2 eggs
1 teaspoon vanilla extract
2 cups sifted flour
1 teaspoon baking powder
1/2 cup chopped
   dark chocolate
1/2 cup chopped
   Marcona almonds

CHOCOLATE-CHUNK MARCONA ALMOND COOKIES

To prepare the cookies: reheat the oven to 325 degrees F. In a mixer fitted with a metal bowl and paddle attachment, cream the butter and sugars together. On low speed, slowly add the eggs and vanilla, and incorporate. With mixer running, add flour and baking powder, and process until dough forms. Do not overmix. Add the chocolate and almonds, and incorporate. Form the dough into 1-1/2-inch balls and arrange on a parchment-lined baking sheet approximately 2 inches apart. Bake for 18 minutes, turning the pan once at the halfway point. Remove from oven and cool cookies on a wire rack.

1/2 pound butter
2 cups packed brown sugar
1-1/2 cups sugar
4 eggs
1 tablespoon vanilla extract
1 tablespoon water
3 cups flour
1/2 cup cocoa
1/4 cup ground pepitas
1 teaspoon salt
1/2 teaspoon ground chipotle
8 ounces dark chocolate, chopped
3 ounces Ibarra chocolate, chopped

TRIPLE CHOCOLATE COOKIES

To prepare the cookies: preheat oven to 325 degrees F. In an electric mixer with the paddle attachment, cream the butter and the sugars together. Add the eggs, vanilla, and water, and continue to mix. Add the flour, cocoa, pepitas, salt, and chipotle, and mix into dough. Remove from the mixer and fold chopped chocolates in by hand with a rubber spatula. Form the dough into 1-1/2-inch balls and arrange on a parchment-lined sheet pan at least 2 inches apart. Bake for 15 minutes; let cool on a wire rack.

1 cup butter
3/4 cup sugar
3/4 cup packed brown sugar
2 eggs
1/4 teaspoon cinnamon
1/4 teaspoon cardamom
1/4 teaspoon salt
1/2 teaspoon nutmeg
1 teaspoon baking soda
1-1/2 cups sifted flour
3/4 pound quinoa flakes
1 cup dried cranberries

QUINOA CRANBERRY COOKIES

To prepare the cookies: preheat the oven to 325 degrees F. In an electric mixer with a paddle attachment, cream the butter and the sugars together. Add the eggs, cinnamon, cardamom, salt, and nutmeg; continue to mix. Whisk the baking soda into the flour and add to mixture along with the quinoa flakes. Remove from the mixer and fold in cranberries by hand with a rubber spatula. Form the dough into 1-1/2-inch balls and arrange on a parchment-lined baking sheet at least 2 inches apart; bake for 15 minutes and cool on a wire rack.

BREAKFAST BECKONS

The Snow Man

We like days when the snow drives in,

From every way, and shuts us in

The house. For then we have good eats,

Like popcorn balls, and mixed nut meats

In fudge, and cakes and other sweets.

We watch the snow as it floats past,

We'll make that snow man of snow at last;

So fat and sleek, and cold clear through,

He'll look just like our bankers do.

Jessa Eula Wallis, Laramie, 1923

IN HIS CLASSIC FLY-FISHING TOME *The Compleat Angler*, Izaak Walton waxed poetic about "a good, honest, wholesome, hungry breakfast." Indeed, the great outdoors and a hearty breakfast seem to go hand in hand; perhaps that's why breakfast has been called the most important meal of the day.

For owner Ron Harrison, the morning meal has always been an integral part of the guest experience at the Rusty Parrot Lodge. Long before sunrise, the aromas of freshly brewed coffee and just-baked muffins begin to waft through the inn, awakening guests to the pleasures ahead. As they make their way to the Wild Sage gathering room for the morning's first cup of coffee, guests find a sideboard laden with healthy offerings: an assortment of fruits and berries, crunchy granola, fresh-squeezed juices, and creamy yogurt. But most diners find it hard to resist the made-to-order daily breakfast specials that are written on the blackboard each morning. Two choices are usually offered, and it's not unusual for guests to struggle with the decision.

While early settlers might have packed a batch of sturdy "johnny cakes" in their saddlebags, the tender, fluffy flapjacks that the Wild Sage chef prepares are served hot off the griddle and accompanied by fresh huckleberries or barrel-aged maple syrup. Grilled flatiron steaks are thinly sliced and presented with crisp-tender roasted fingerling potatoes and sundried tomato-leek butter. Waffles are studded with crunchy pecans and served with a decadent bananas flambé, and French toast is dipped in a Grand Marnier–infused batter and fried to a golden brown. Even popular diner fare such as biscuits and gravy gets an update at the Wild Sage with fluffy, just-baked buttermilk biscuits enlivened with jalapeños and topped with a generous serving of hearty, buffalo chipotle sausage gravy.

With a good, honest, wholesome breakfast under their belts, guests are ready for whatever adventures the day brings—whether they're headed off to ski, hike, bike, kayak, fish, or simply explore the shops and galleries in the charming town of Jackson.

MAKES 6 SERVINGS

FOR THE CRÈME ANGLAISE

1 cup heavy cream
1 vanilla bean, split and scraped
Pinch of salt
3 egg yolks
1/4 cup sugar
2 tablespoons maple syrup

FOR THE FRENCH TOAST

3 eggs
1 cup heavy cream
1/2 cup sugar
1 tablespoon finely chopped
    orange zest
2 tablespoons Grand Marnier
1 vanilla bean
12 (1-inch-thick) slices dry French
    baguette

FOR THE COULIS

6 blood oranges, squeezed
    to make 1 cup juice
1/3 cup sugar
Pinch of salt

FOR THE GARNISH

3 blood oranges
1 cup whipped cream

GRAND MARNIER FRENCH TOAST
with Blood Orange Coulis, Maple Crème Anglaise, and Orange Supremes

The blood orange is a small, juicy orange variety that has a deep crimson fruit inside. It is less acidic but a little more bitter than common oranges, and this recipe pairs the juice, zest, and segments of the fruit with a rich, sweet French toast— all enlivened with a shot of Grand Marnier liqueur.

To prepare the crème anglaise: combine the cream, vanilla bean, and salt in a medium saucepan, and scald the cream (heat to the point where tiny bubbles form around the edges, but do not allow it to boil). In a metal mixing bowl, beat together the egg yolks and sugar until light yellow. Slowly add a little of the cream mixture and whisk vigorously to temper the yolks; add the rest of the mixture and whisk until combined. In the top of a double boiler, cook the mixture, stirring constantly, until it reaches 175 degrees F and will coat the back of a spoon. Add the maple syrup, strain, and chill in the refrigerator.

To prepare the French toast: combine the eggs, cream, sugar, zest, and Grand Marnier in a metal mixing bowl. Split the vanilla bean and scrape the seeds into the mixture; discard the pod and whisk batter until blended. Let stand for 1 hour. Reserve the baguette slices until ready to finish the French toast.

To prepare the coulis: combine all the ingredients in a small saucepan and cook over medium-high heat until the mixture is reduced and becomes syrupy. Remove from heat, strain, set aside, and keep warm.

To prepare the garnish: use a zester to remove the zest from the oranges. Next, use a sharp peeler to remove the peel and white pitch from the oranges. Carefully slice in between the connective membranes to remove the segments (or "supremes"). Set aside the zest and supremes.

To finish the French toast: brush an electric griddle with cooking oil and heat to 350 degrees F. Soak the bread slices in the batter for 4 minutes, turning several times to make sure they are evenly soaked. Cook the French toast until golden brown on both sides.

To serve the breakfast: arrange 2 slices of French toast in the center of each plate. Pour some of the coulis and crème anglaise around the toast. Garnish with the reserved blood orange supremes, zest, and whipped cream.

MAKES 8 SERVINGS

FOR THE GLAZE

1/2 cup packed brown sugar
1/4 teaspoon vanilla extract
2 tablespoons warm water

FOR THE CAKE

1/2 cup butter, softened
1 vanilla bean, split and scraped
1-1/2 cups packed brown sugar
2 eggs
1-1/2 cups yogurt
2 cups flour
1 cup chopped pecans
1 teaspoon baking soda
1 teaspoon ground cinnamon
1/2 teaspoon salt

FOR THE CRUMBLE

1/2 cup packed brown sugar
1/2 cup flour
1/2 teaspoon ground cinnamon
4 tablespoons butter, softened

CRUMBLE-TOPPED PECAN COFFEE CAKE
with Brown Sugar Drizzle

Perfect with a cup of the Wild Sage's cappuccino, this easy-to-make coffee cake is covered with both a crumbly, buttery crumb topping and a sweet caramel glaze.

To prepare the glaze: combine all the ingredients in a small metal bowl and mix well, let stand for 1 hour.

To prepare the cake: preheat the oven to 340 degrees F. Prepare a 9-inch springform pan by lining the bottom with parchment paper; apply cooking spray on the bottom and sides, and then dust with flour. In a large metal mixing bowl, combine the butter, vanilla, and sugar. Slowly add the eggs to the mixture, mixing well to incorporate. Add the yogurt and fold in until smooth. Combine the remaining dry ingredients in a food processor fitted with a metal blade and process until the nuts are finely ground. Slowly sift the dry ingredients into the egg mixture. Spoon the mixture into the springform pan and tap lightly on the counter so it all settles evenly.

To prepare the crumble: combine all the ingredients in a metal mixing bowl. Mix well until mixture becomes crumbly. Sprinkle the entire mixture over the top of the cake. Bake for 50–55 minutes in the oven, or until a toothpick inserted in the middle comes out clean. Remove from the oven and let cool for 15 minutes. Top with the glaze and cut into equal portions.

MAKES 4 TO 6 SERVINGS

FOR THE SAUSAGE

2 chipotle peppers in adobo sauce
2 cloves garlic, peeled and minced
1/2 teaspoon salt
4 sun-dried tomatoes, minced
3/4 pound finely ground 70/30
    buffalo meat

FOR THE GRAVY

1 tablespoon canola oil
4 tablespoons flour
1-1/2 cups chicken stock
1 cup cream
1/2 teaspoon salt
1/4 teaspoon black pepper

FOR THE BISCUITS

1 cup flour
1 tablespoon baking powder
Pinch of salt
1/3 cup butter
2/3 cup buttermilk
1 jalapeño, seeded and brunoised
1/2 cup grated jalapeño Jack cheese

GARNISH

Fresh chives

JALAPEÑO BUTTERMILK BISCUITS
with Buffalo Chipotle Sausage Gravy

Forget the truck-stop version of biscuits and gravy; the Wild Sage re-creates the stick-to-your-ribs favorite with cheesy jalapeño-studded biscuits topped with a hearty gravy enlivened with house-made buffalo sausage.

To prepare the sausage: combine the chipotle, garlic, salt, and tomatoes in a food processor and process until finely ground. Add the meat and pulse until combined; Set aside.

To prepare the gravy: cook the sausage mixture with the oil in a large sauté pan over medium-high heat until cooked through, about 6 minutes. Add the flour and cook until the mixture thickens and is lightly browned. Add the stock and cream, bring to a simmer, and cook until thickened. Season with salt and pepper; set aside and keep warm.

To prepare the biscuits: preheat the oven to 350 degrees F. Mix the flour, baking powder, and salt in the bowl of an electric mixer. Add the butter and beat with a paddle on low until the butter is in pea-sized pieces. Add the buttermilk, jalapeño, and cheese, and mix until incorporated. Place on a floured workspace and roll out the dough to a 1 inch thickness. Cut with a round cutter, transfer to a greased baking sheet, and bake until golden brown, about 25 minutes. Cool on a wire rack.

To serve the biscuits and gravy: split open the hot biscuits and place on the center of a plate. Ladle the gravy over the biscuits and garnish with chives.

MAKES 6 SERVINGS

FOR THE WAFFLES

1/2 cup chopped pecans
2 eggs
1/2 teaspoon vanilla extract
1-1/4 cups milk
1 cup flour
1 teaspoon baking powder
Pinch of salt
1/4 cup butter, melted

FOR THE BANANAS

4 tablespoons butter
6 niño bananas, peeled
    and halved lengthwise
2 tablespoons brown sugar
2 tablespoons dark rum
2 tablespoons Frangelico liqueur
1/4 teaspoon cinnamon

FOR THE CREMA

1 cup heavy cream
2 tablespoons powdered sugar
1/4 teaspoon cinnamon
1/4 teaspoon vanilla extract

PECAN WAFFLES
with Niño Bananas Flambé
and Cinnamon Crema

Bananas flambé for breakfast? The Wild Sage cooks pull out
all the stops with this popular offering, which pairs crunchy
pecan waffles with warm bananas—yes, they're flaming—in
a rum-based caramel sauce.

To prepare the waffle batter: in a food processor fitted with a metal blade, process the pecans until finely ground. In a metal mixing bowl, combine eggs, vanilla, and milk. Using a rubber spatula, fold the dry ingredients into the wet portion. Add the melted butter. Do not overmix. Set aside until ready to finish waffles.

To prepare the bananas: melt the butter in a sauté pan over medium heat. Add bananas and sauté for 1 minute. Add the sugar and swirl to combine. Pull the pan away from the heat, add the liquor, return to the heat, and flame off the alcohol. Add cinnamon, set aside, and keep warm.

To prepare the crema: whisk the cream in a chilled metal mixing bowl to incorporate air. Once the cream holds stiff peaks, add the sugar, cinnamon, and vanilla. Continue to whisk until all ingredients are combined. Chill.

To finish the waffles: preheat a waffle iron. Apply nonstick spray to cooking surface and cook waffles according to manufacturer's directions.

To serve the breakfast: place a waffle in the center of each plate. Top with some of the bananas and sauce. Finish the plate with a large dollop of crema.

MAKES 6 SERVINGS

FOR THE SAUCE

1 small yellow onion, peeled and
   roughly chopped
2 cups peeled, chopped plum tomatoes
1 cup water
2 jalapeños, seeded and roughly
   chopped
4 cloves garlic, peeled and chopped
1/4 teaspoon lime juice
1/4 teaspoon salt
2 tablespoons packed chopped
   cilantro

FOR THE CHILAQUILES

4 ounces yellow corn tortilla chips
3/4 pound bulk chorizo sausage,
   cooked and cooled
10 ounces chicken breast, cooked
   and shredded
6 ounces Cotija cheese

ROASTED ORGANIC CHICKEN AND CHORIZO SAUSAGE CHILAQUILES

Chilaquiles are a traditional Mexican dish of baked, fried

corn tortilla strips. The Wild Sage adds spicy chorizo

sausage and tender chicken to the mix, topping it with

a fresh tomato-cilantro sauce.

To prepare the sauce: combine all the ingredients except the cilantro in a medium saucepan and simmer for 30 minutes. Add the cilantro and remove from the heat. Working in batches, process the sauce in a blender until smooth. Set aside.

To prepare the chilaquiles: preheat the oven to 300 degrees F and lightly grease a 9 x 4-inch loaf pan. Place a thin layer of sauce in the bottom of the pan and then put a layer of tortilla chips over the sauce. Top the chips with a third of the chorizo, chicken, and cheese. Repeat the layering process two more times. Cook the mixture in the oven for 20 minutes. Let the chilaquiles cool for 10 minutes before slicing into equal portions. The dish can also be served with eggs of your choice.

MAKES 6 SERVINGS

FOR THE SAUCE

3 Roma tomatoes

3 cloves garlic

1 shallot, peeled and minced

1 jalapeño, seeded and minced

2 cups water

1/4 teaspoon salt

1/2 bunch cilantro, stems removed

FOR THE PICO DE GALLO

4 Roma tomatoes, cored and diced
  (1/4-inch cubes)

1 shallot, peeled and brunoised

2 tablespoons cilantro
  chiffonade

1/4 teaspoon salt

1/4 teaspoon fresh lime juice

2 jalapeños, seeded and brunoised

**FOR THE FILLING
AND GARNISH**

1 cup black beans, cooked and
  drained

12 ounces chorizo sausage, sliced
  and browned

2 tablespoons butter

12 eggs

1 avocado

3 ounces queso fresco, rumbled

6 (8-inch) flour tortillas

HUEVOS RANCHEROS
with Chorizo Sausage, Pico De Gallo, and Queso Fresco

This is a classic Mexican breakfast, and the Wild Sage makes fresh pico de gallo and a spicy black-bean and chorizo sausage filling to top the flour tortillas and fried eggs, which are accompanied by authentic queso fresco and cool avocado.

To prepare the sauce: combine all ingredients except the cilantro in a saucepan and cook over medium-high heat until reduced by half. Remove from heat and steep the cilantro for 10 minutes. Remove the cilantro and process sauce in a blender until smooth. Set the sauce in a warm area of the kitchen until ready to serve.

To prepare the pico de gallo: combine all the ingredients in a small bowl and refrigerate for 1 hour.

To prepare the filling and garnish: preheat the oven to 375 degrees F. In a sauté pan heat the sauce and add the black beans and chorizo sausage. In a separate nonstick pan, heat the butter until foam subsides, and then cook eggs over easy. Peel and pit the avocado, and slice into 6 wedges; slice each wedge into a fan.

To serve the breakfast: heat the tortillas in the oven until warm and pliable. Place one tortilla per plate and spoon a sixth of the mixture onto the center of each tortilla. Top with two eggs, pico de gallo, queso fresco, and one fanned avocado wedge.

Homemade Fig Jam

When ripe figs are in season, the Wild Sage chefs prepare this rich, dense fig jam. A staple of Mediterranean cuisine, the preserve tastes delicious on a slice of crusty bread or toast, or served with cheese and crispy crostini.

Photo credit: Stock Photo

MAKES APPROXIMATELY
1 CUP

1 pound ripe figs, quartered
3 cups water
1 cup sugar

To prepare the jam: combine all the ingredients in a heavy saucepan and bring to a boil over medium-high heat. Simmer, stirring often, until the mixture is reduced by half. Remove from the heat and run through a fine meshed food mill. Refrigerate and use within 7 days.

MAKES 4 TO 6 SERVINGS

FOR THE SALMON

1-1/2 teaspoons coarsely cracked
black pepper
2 tablespoons coarse sea salt
2 tablespoons brown sugar
2 tablespoons chopped
fennel fronds
1 pound wild-caught sockeye
salmon, skin on
2 tablespoons Sambuca liqueur

FOR THE CRÈME FRAÎCHE

1 tablespoon buttermilk
1 cup heavy cream
1 tablespoon microplaned
lemon zest

FOR THE POTATO RÖSTI

2 tablespoons canola oil
2 russet potatoes, peeled and
julienned (1/8-inch pieces)
1/2 teaspoon salt
1/4 teaspoon freshly ground black
pepper

FOR THE HASH

2 tablespoons red onion brunoise
2 tablespoons capers, rinsed
1/2 tablespoon finely chopped dill
2 teaspoons fresh lemon juice
2 tablespoons diced Roma tomato
(1/4-inch cubes)

BROWN SUGAR– AND SAMBUCA-CURED SALMON HASH
with Potato Rösti and Lemon Crème Fraîche

Breakfast hash was originally created as a way for the kitchen to use leftovers, but the Wild Sage reinvents the dish with wild-caught salmon accompanied by fried potatoes, fresh dill, and a lemony cream sauce.

To prepare the salmon: combine all of the ingredients for the marinade except the salmon and Sambuca in a small mixing bowl. Rub the mixture on the salmon and coat evenly. Cover tightly in a nonreactive pan and refrigerate. Pour the Sambuca on the salmon after 24 hours and continue to "cure" for a total time of 48–72 hours.

To prepare the crème fraîche: combine the buttermilk and cream in a metal mixing bowl and mix well. Let stand loosely covered overnight at room temperature. Next day, add the lemon zest and refrigerate for 3 hours. Using a wire whisk, whip the cream until light and fluffy.

To prepare the rösti: heat the oil in a nonstick sauté pan. Place a 3-inch metal ring mold in the bottom of the pan. Spoon a "nest" of potatoes in the mold, about 3/4 inch thick. Cook over medium-high heat for 6 minutes, or until golden. Flip and cook the other side until golden; season with salt and pepper. Remove from the heat and unmold, drain on a tray lined with paper towels, set aside, and keep warm. Repeat with the rest of the potatoes.

To prepare the hash: remove the salmon from the marinade and pat it dry. Cut into 1/4-inch dice. Toss the salmon with all of the hash ingredients and let marinate for 20 minutes.

To serve the breakfast: place a potato rösti in the center of each plate and top with some of the hash mixture. Use two spoons to make a quenelle of the crème fraîche and place on the side.

MAKES 5 SERVINGS

FOR THE SAUSAGE

1 Fuji apple, diced (1/4-inch cubes)

1 tablespoon canola oil

2 (6-ounce) boneless chicken
    breasts, trimmed of fat and
    sinew

1 tablespoon minced fresh tarragon

1/2 teaspoon salt

1/4 teaspoon pepper

1 quart water

1 teaspoon salt

2 tablespoons butter

FOR THE OMELET

3 cups spinach

15 eggs (3 eggs per omelet)

2-1/2 tablespoons butter, divided

12 ounces chicken sausage,
    browned (see above)

1 cup grated St. Andre cheese

CHICKEN AND ROASTED APPLE SAUSAGE OMELET
with St. Andres Cheese and Baby Spinach

A delicate homemade sausage of chicken, Fuji apple, and seasonings is the star of this savory omelet, paired with tender spinach and cheese.

To prepare the sausage: preheat the oven to 350 degrees F. In a small bowl, toss the apple in the oil, spread on a small baking sheet, and roast for 25 minutes. Meanwhile, in a food processor fitted with a metal blade, process the chicken until it resembles a coarse paste. Transfer to a metal mixing bowl and use a rubber spatula to fold in the tarragon, salt, and pepper. Divide the mixture in half and roll into two cylinders, each approximately 1 inch in diameter; wrap tightly with two layers of plastic wrap, tying off the ends. In a large saucepan over medium-high heat, bring the water and salt to a boil. Poach the sausages for 10 minutes and let rest for an additional 3 minutes. Remove the plastic wrap and slice the sausage into 1/2-inch slices. Heat the butter in a sauté pan over medium-high heat and brown the sausage slices quickly on both sides; reserve warm.

To prepare the omelet: preheat a small 8-inch nonstick pan over medium heat. Add the spinach to the pan and cook until it is wilted; set aside and wipe the pan. Return to heat and cook 3 beaten eggs per omelet, using 1/2 tablespoon of butter per omelet. Cook the first side using a rubber spatula to move the eggs around the pan and cook evenly. Flip over and add a fifth each of the spinach, sausage, and cheese. Cook until warmed, fold over, and serve.

MAKES 4 SERVINGS

FOR THE SYRUP

1 cup bourbon
1 cup 100-percent
     maple syrup

FOR THE JOHNNY CAKES

3 cups water
1 teaspoon vanilla extract
1 cup white cornmeal
1 egg
3/8 cup heavy cream
1 cup flour
1/4 teaspoon salt
4 tablespoons butter

FOR THE GARNISH

1/2 cup fresh-picked mountain
     huckleberries
Powdered sugar for dusting

JOHNNY CAKES
with Bourbon-Infused Maple Syrup
and Mountain Huckleberries

The secret to the Wild Sage's tender johnny cakes is a dash of heavy cream; the cornmeal-based pancakes are served hot off the griddle with fresh Wyoming huckleberries and a tantalizing bourbon and maple syrup blend.

To prepare the syrup: cook the bourbon in a small tall-sided saucepan over medium-heat until it is reduced by 90 percent. (Be careful that the bourbon does not ignite.) Add the maple syrup to the pan and bring to a simmer. Remove from direct heat, set aside and keep warm.

To prepare the johnny cakes: bring the water and vanilla extract to a boil in a small saucepan over high heat. Pour the cornmeal in a metal mixing bowl and add the water mixture; stir and let stand for 30 minutes. Add the egg, cream, flour, and salt to the cornmeal mixture; stir until well combined.

Preheat a flat griddle to 350 degrees F. Working in batches, melt some of the butter on the griddle and ladle the batter into thin 4-inch circles. Cook until the pancakes become slightly golden and small bubbles form, then flip and cook the other side until lightly browned, about 1 minute.

To serve the breakfast: arrange 3 cakes per person on a plate and top with warm syrup and huckleberries. Dust with powdered sugar.

MAKES 4 SERVINGS

FOR THE SAUCE

3/4 cup heavy cream

1/4 cup chicken stock

2 cloves garlic, peeled and minced

1 shallot, peeled and minced

3 ounces (18-month-aged) white
    cheddar, grated*

FOR THE CROQUE MADAME

1/2 pound Jambon de Paris or Black
    Forest ham, thinly sliced

2 tablespoons butter, softened

4 slices challah, cut into 3/4-inch-
    thick rounds

3 tablespoons clarified butter

4 eggs

GARNISH

1 tablespoon finely chopped parsley

*The Wild Sage kitchen uses a
bandage-wrapped aged white cheddar
made from raw whole milk.

CROQUE MADAME
with Jambon de Paris, Fried Egg, and Aged Cheddar Mornay

A variation of the popular Croque Monsieur sandwich, this breakfast version pairs eggs and thinly sliced ham with fresh challah bread. The sandwich is grilled to a crispy brown and smothered with cheesy Mornay sauce.

To prepare the sauce: heat the cream, stock, garlic, and
shallot in a small saucepan. Reduce the mixture by
one-third. Pour the grated cheese into the mixture and mix
well with a wire whisk until fully melted and incorporated.
Strain the mixture through a fine mesh sieve, set aside,
and keep warm.

To prepare the Croque Madame: preheat an electric
griddle to 350 degrees F. Sear the ham to remove excess
water and brown lightly; drain on a platter lined with paper
towels. Butter the challah rounds on both sides and grill
until golden brown; set aside. Brush the clarified butter
on the griddle and cook the eggs to your preference.

To serve the breakfast: top each slice of challah with the
ham and egg, and repeat with the other three rounds. Top
the open-faced sandwiches with a spoonful of the Mornay
Sauce and sprinkle with the parsley.

MAKES 6 SERVINGS

FOR THE BUTTER

1 leek, chopped
   (white part only)
1 tablespoon canola oil
10 sun-dried tomatoes in oil, diced
   (1/4-inch cubes, about 1 cup)
1/4 teaspoon salt
1 tablespoon finely
   chopped parsley
1/2 cup butter, softened

FOR THE POTATOES

18 new red potatoes,
   scrubbed and quartered
2 tablespoons canola oil
1 teaspoon salt
1/2 teaspoon freshly ground black
   pepper

FOR THE STEAKS

2 tablespoons canola oil
6 (4-ounce) flatiron steaks
2 teaspoons salt
1 teaspoon freshly ground black
   pepper

FOR THE EGGS

1 tablespoon butter
12 eggs
1 teaspoon salt
1 teaspoon black pepper

FLATIRON STEAK AND EGGS
with Roasted New Potatoes and Sun-Dried Tomato–Leek Butter

The flatiron steak is a cut of meat from the shoulder of the steer that is considered to be second in tenderness only to the tenderloin. The Wild Sage pan-sears the steaks and serves them topped with a melting pat of compound butter accompanied by crispy new potatoes and fried eggs.

To prepare the butter: sweat the leek in the oil in a sauté pan over medium heat until translucent. Transfer to a separate container and cool in the refrigerator. Fold the leek mixture, tomatoes, salt, and parsley into the softened butter and mix well to combine. On a flat surface, wrap the butter in parchment to form a log shape, twisting it at the end, and refrigerate. The butter can be frozen for up to 3 weeks.

To prepare the potatoes: preheat the oven to 325 degrees F. Toss the potatoes in the oil, salt, and pepper, and roast for 40 minutes, turning occasionally; set aside and keep warm.

To prepare the steak: heat the oil in a sauté pan over medium-high heat. Season the steaks on both sides with salt and pepper, and sear on each side. Finish in a preheated 400 degree F oven for 3–5 minutes. Let the meat rest for 4–6 minutes.

To prepare the eggs: in a nonstick pan, heat the butter over medium heat and cook the eggs over easy; season with salt and pepper.

To serve the breakfast: remove the butter from the refrigerator and slice off 6 (1/4-inch-thick) rounds. Turn the broiler to high. Slice each steak against the grain into four slices, and top each with the 1 round of butter. Quickly melt the butter on the steaks under the broiler. On each plate arrange 1 steak with 2 eggs and a side of potatoes.

MAKES 24 MUFFINS

1/3 cup canola oil
4 eggs
2 teaspoons vanilla extract
1 cup vanilla yogurt
4 tablespoons butter, melted
1/4 cup orange juice
2 oranges, finely zested
   on a microplane
3-1/4 cups flour
1 cup sugar
1 teaspoon baking powder
1/2 teaspoon baking soda
1/2 teaspoon salt
1 cup sun-dried cranberries

CRANBERRY AND ORANGE MUFFINS

Orange zest and sweet-sour dried cranberries flavor a batch of the Wild Sage's popular muffins, which were inspired by Ron Harrison's grandmother's recipe. The secret to their tender texture is the addition of yogurt to the batter and the chef's reminder to stir just until combined.

To prepare the muffins: preheat the oven to 350 degrees F and line a muffin pan with paper liners. In a large metal mixing bowl, use a rubber spatula to combine the oil, eggs, vanilla, yogurt, butter, orange juice, and zest. In a separate bowl, combine the flour, sugar, baking powder, baking soda, and salt. Sift the dry ingredients into the egg mixture and stir just until combined. Gently fold in the cranberries. Fill each muffin liner 3/4 full and bake for 23 minutes, or until lightly browned and a toothpick inserted in the center comes out clean. Let cool briefly on a wire rack before removing from the pan.

MAKES 8 SERVINGS

FOR THE CRUST

3/4 cup flour
Pinch of salt
4 tablespoons butter
2 tablespoons cold water

FOR THE FILLING

1 tablespoon canola oil
2/3 cup diced onion
    (1/4-inch cubes)
1/2 cup peeled, seeded,
    and finely chopped
    poblano chiles
1/4 pound Kurobuta ham, diced
    (1/4-inch cubes)
4 eggs
1/2 teaspoon salt
1 cup half-and-half
1 cup finely grated Cabot white
    cheddar cheese

DENVER QUICHE
with Kurobuta Ham, Cabot White Cheddar Cheese, and Poblano Chiles

Borrowing from the popular Denver omelet, this tender quiche is chock-full of tasty additions: white cheddar cheese, ham, onions, and spicy poblano chiles.

To prepare the crust: preheat the oven to 325 degrees F. In the bowl of an electric mixer, combine the flour, salt, and butter until pea-sized clumps form. Slowly add the water, a couple of drops at a time, until dough forms. Remove from bowl, wrap in plastic wrap, and refrigerate for 30 minutes. Lightly flour a clean, dry flat surface and roll the dough to a 1/4 inch thickness. Drape the dough into a 9-inch quiche pan and mold to fit, leaving extra dough at top of pan to accommodate shrinkage. Lightly poke the bottom with a fork and bake for 10 minutes. If any pockets form, lightly tap down; cool on a wire rack.

To prepare the filling: heat the oil in a sauté pan over moderate heat and add the onion; cook until browned and caramelized. Add the chiles and cook for 3 minutes; add the ham. In a metal mixing bowl, use a whisk to combine the eggs, salt, and half-and-half. Spoon the ham mixture into the cooked crust, sprinkle with the cheese and pour the egg mixture over the top. Bake for about 1 hour, or until the eggs are cooked and the center is puffed and golden brown. Let cool for 20 minutes before serving.

MAKES 5 SERVINGS

FOR THE PESTO

1/2 cup gently packed
   cilantro leaves
1/4 cup canola oil
1/8 teaspoon salt
1/4 teaspoon lemon juice

FOR THE GRITS

4 cups water
1 teaspoon salt
1 cup grits
1/2 cup grated Asadero cheese
1 jalapeño, seeded and brunoised
1 Roma tomato, diced
   (1/4-inch cubes)

FOR THE CHILE RELLENOS

5 pasilla chiles, skinned
   and seeded
10 ounces lump crabmeat
1/2 cup grated Asadero cheese

FOR THE GARNISH

1 medium Roma tomato,
   diced (1/4-inch cubes)

CHILE RELLENO
with Asadero Cheese Grits, Lump Crab, and Cilantro Pesto

Pasilla chiles are stuffed with crabmeat and cheesy grits in this ultimate breakfast version of Mexican chile rellenos. The dish is topped with a fresh, house-made cilantro pesto.

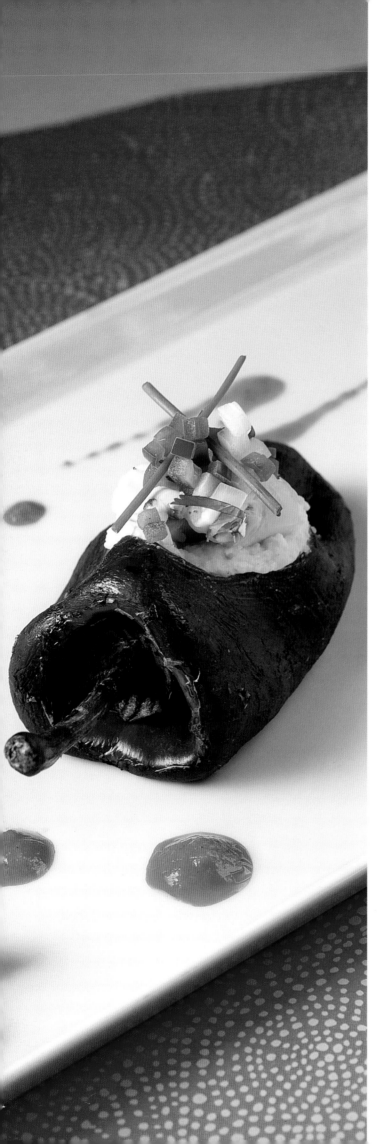

To prepare the pesto: combine the cilantro and oil in a blender and process for 20 seconds. Add the salt and lemon juice, pulse briefly, and set aside at room temperature.

To prepare the grits: bring the water and salt to a boil in a saucepan over medium-high heat. Add the grits and stir constantly until cooked and the mixture is thickened. Remove from the heat and fold in the cheese; cool slightly and fold in the jalapeño and tomato.

To prepare the rellenos: preheat the oven to 350 degrees F. Stuff each pepper with some of the grits mixture, about 3/4 full. Top the grits with 2 ounces of the lump crab. Finish off with a topping of cheese. Stuff the rest of the peppers in the same fashion. Place the peppers on a baking sheet that has been sprayed with nonstick spray and bake for 15 minutes, or until the cheese is fully melted and just starting to brown.

To serve the breakfast: place a relleno in the center of the plate. Garnish with the tomato and drizzle some of the pesto around each pepper.

Source Directory

ASIAN INGREDIENTS

Asian Food Grocer
131 West Harris Avenue
South San Francisco, CA 94080
(888) 482-2742
www.asianfoodgrocer.com
For Asian spices, seasonings, and specialty foods

BAKING INGREDIENTS

King Arthur Flour
58 Billings Farm Road
White River Junction, VT 05001
(800) 827-6836
www.kingarthurflour.com
For specialty flours, bakeware and tools

CHEESES

Zingerman's Mail Order
422 Detroit Street
Ann Arbor, MI 48104
(888) 636-8162
www.zingermans.com
For Humboldt Fog and other specialty cheeses

FLAVORINGS

Terra Sonoma Food Company
P.O. Box 444
Geyserville, CA 95441
(707) 431-1382
www.terrasonoma.com
*For verjus, a natural flavoring enhancer made from
the tart, unfermented juice of unripe wine grapes*

GRAINS

Eden Foods
701 Tecumseh Road
Clinton, MI 49236
(888) 424-3336
www.edenfoods.com/store/
For quinoa and other organic grains

GREENS

Planet Earth Diversified
165 Earth Way Drive
Suite Red Barn 1
Stanardsville, VA 22973
(434) 985-3570
www.planetearthdiversified.com
For microgreens, herbs, edible flowers,
wheatgrass and gourmet lettuces

MEATS

GermanDeli.com
5100 Hwy 121
Colleyville, TX 76034
(877) 437-6269
www.germandeli.com
For speck ham, a dry-cured ham with an intense flavor

Montana Legend
1353 Old Tennessee Road, Ste 121
Corona, CA 92881
(951) 284-4202
www.montanalegend.com
For premium Angus beef

Prairie Harvest
P.O. Box 1013
Spearfish, SD 57783
(800) 350-7166
www.prairieharvest.com
For large and small wild game, poultry, and game birds

POULTRY

Debragga and Spitler
826-D Washington Street
New York, NY 10014
www.debragga.com
For Moulard duck legs and heritage-breed
free-range poultry

SEAFOOD

Bristol Bay Seafood
P.O. Box 4539
1200 Gregory Lane #2
Jackson, WY 83001
www.bristolbaysalmon.com
(888) 532-3892
For fresh-flown wild, natural, and sustainable seafood

SPICES

Savory Spice Shop
1537 Platte Street
Denver, CO 80202
(303) 477-3322
www. savoryspiceshop.com
For a wide variety of freshly ground and whole spices

RESOURCES

The authors gratefully acknowledge the following books and websites used as resources for this book:

A Place Called Jackson Hole, A Historic Resource Study of Grand Teton National Park by John Daughterty, with contributions by Stephanie Crockett, William H. Goetzmann, Reynold G. Jackson, Grand Teton National Park, National Park Service Intermountain Region, published by Grand Teton National Park Association, 1999.

National Elk Refuge
www.fws.gov/nationalelkrefuge

Grand Teton National Park
www.nps.gov/grte/

INDEX

METRIC CONVERSION CHART

LIQUID AND DRY MEASURES			TEMPERATURE CONVERSION CHART	
U.S.	Canadian	Australian	Fahrenheit	Celsius
1/4 teaspoon	1 mL	1 ml	250	120
1/2 teaspoon	2 mL	2 ml	275	140
1 teaspoon	5 mL	5 ml	300	150
1 tablespoon	15 mL	20 ml	325	160
1/4 cup	50 mL	60 ml	350	180
1/3 cup	75 mL	80 ml	375	190
1/2 cup	125 mL	125 ml	400	200
2/3 cup	150 mL	170 ml	425	220
3/4 cup	175 mL	190 ml	450	230
1 cup	250 mL	250 ml	475	240
1 quart	1 liter	1 litre	500	260